RODERICK
FRASER
WILLETT

The Good Shot

MOONRAKER PRESS

TO CATHERINE

© 1979 Roderick Fraser Willett & Moonraker Press
First published in 1979 by Moonraker Press
26 St Margarets Street, Bradford-on-Avon, Wiltshire
SBN 239.00186.9
Printed by T. H. Brickell & Son Ltd,
The Blackmore Press, Shaftesbury, Dorset,
and bound in England at The Pitman Press, Bath.

contents

list of illustrations

Diagrams drawn by James Hobson

1 an introduction to shotgun shooting

Do you shoot with your father's, or possibly even your grandfather's guns, which have never been altered to fit you, but in your opinion are none the worse for that? Do you, when pressed by your friends, admit to being a fair shot, though of course like everyone else you have your off-days? Do you reckon that in the course of a season, although you do not actually keep a tally, your average of kills to cartridges must certainly be 1 to 3, if not better? You deceive yourself, and you know it.

When discussing the highlights of a day's sport round your host's fireside in the mellow atmosphere engendered by his hospitality, it is so easy to forget, for example, those two abortive shots at a woodpigeon at the beginning of the first drive, or that really high pheasant later on, which you decided was too difficult and pretended not to see, or the wild duck at the end of the day that you palpably botched, was killed by your neighbour, and was certainly not coming down 'anyway', as you have in mind to record in your gamebook. Some good and most bad marksmen have a characteristic in common; every bird they hit, they claim dead. Picking up for such people is a purgatory, whereas when you stand with a good shot who freely admits to a probable runner down, and has a word of praise for your dog when the bird is brought to hand, it is a pleasure. Such a man is also far more congenial company as a fellow gun.

The aim of this book is to help you to become as good a marksman as your natural talents will allow, and also a safe one, because a truly 'good shot' should be as safe as he is skilful. A point on which it helps a novice to be clear is the standard of marksmanship to which he should aspire. In this context the high scores attained in competition clay-pigeon shooting are very misleading. A good game shot, who makes the most of his opportunities, does not kill almost every time he pulls the trigger. Some dedicated clay-pigeon shots may argue that he should, and pour scorn on the comparatively poor results with which even the best game shots appear satisfied. But they forget that like is not being compared with like, and therefore no valid comparison is possible. However, in so far as their criticism implies that many game shots are poorer marksmen than they ought, or need to be, it has substance.

If a game shot is to make the most of his chances, he will have to tackle game nearing the limit of effective range, and avoid wasting ammunition on quarry out of range. He should therefore be aware of this limit, and if he also understands the factors that play a part in deciding it, so much the better.

Even the best shots sometimes have their off-days, as do leading players in first-class cricket. So just as the performance of the latter is adjudged over the course of a season, so should be that of the former. The most thorough assessment of marksmanship in the shooting field which has been placed on record is that made by Sir Ralph Payne-Galleway, Bt, about the beginning of this century. He was one of the leading shots of his day, and had a wealth of experience on which to call. The Table he produced is as under:

Category of Marksman	Head of Game Killed per 100 Cartridges Fired
Inferior Marksman	25
Average Marksman	30
Good Marksman	35
Very Good Marksman	40
First Class Marksman	45

The first reaction of some people may be that the figures in the right-hand column seem rather low, especially in the case of the 'average marksman'. As I have mentioned in the opening paragraphs we all find it easier to remember our hits than our misses. In my experience the better a marksman, the less variable his day-to-day performance, which is probably in part because he seldom misses the simple targets. On the other hand the results obtained by a poor marksman may fluctuate dramatically from those when he qualifies as 'good' to those which he prefers to forget altogether! So if performance is judged over a whole season this Table seems to me to offer sound guidance. It should make clear that it is not such a disgrace to miss as novices are apt to fear. As self-confidence plays such a decisive part in the making of a competent marksman, it is a great help to have this in proper perspective. Emphasis on the importance of good marksmanship is sometimes held to detract from good sportsmanship. This is a fundamental misunderstanding of the point at issue.

The life of a 'rifle' on safari in Africa can be at risk from the quarry he pursues, while that of a 'gun' at a shoot in Britain is not. Before the former takes the field he therefore ensures that he is a reasonably competent marksman, has a properly zeroed rifle, and is using a satisfactory combination of weapon and cartridge to kill his quarry cleanly with one well-aimed shot. A 'rifle' on a Scottish deer forest takes similar measures before setting forth. By comparison the average British 'gun' is extremely casual; only a minority seek instruction in how to shoot; many never have the fit of their gun checked, or test the patterns it shoots on the plate; few bother to acquire even the most elementary knowledge of shotgun ballistics, though many develop strong prejudices about such matters, which more often than not are entirely at variance with reality. A gun should feel no less a duty to his quarry than a rifle to be a reasonably competent and knowledgeable shot, even though his personal safety may not be dependent on it. To fail in this repsect seems to me a failing in sportsmanship.

Game shooting is a recreation, and as such is meant to be enjoyed. But as it involves taking creatures' lives we should treat it more seriously than if it were merely a matter of thrashing a ball round a golf course. East Anglia has long been regarded as the 'Mecca' of English shooting. The late Arthur Street once wrote that when shooting there, he always felt his host would rather a guest seduced his wife than tailed his pheasants. Though a little extreme, this conveys the right idea.

When an aspiring shot begins to realise how much he enjoys his sport and take a lively interest in all its aspects, one of his ambitions will almost certainly be to become as fine a marksman as he can. This is admirable provided he understands that learning the appropriate safety drills and etiquette is an integral part of his education to this end, and that it should be equally a normal reflex action to check whether or not a gun is loaded as soon as he lays hands on it as to thumb forward the safety catch when he mounts his gun to take a shot. The older a novice the more practice that may be necessary to make this so, because actions which quickly become instinctive with a young person take much longer to do so with a man in middle age.

Insistence on really high standards of safety in the shooting field has declined in the past 30 years. If a qualified and unbiased observer were asked to check on the safety drill of the guns on any shoot selected at random in this country, I would be surprised if by the day's end at least 75 per cent of them had not incurred penalty points. The onset of the shooting-season in the U.S.A. reputedly heralds in an annual blood-bath. At least we are spared that in Britain, though shooting accidents still occur every year. It is only by teaching proper safety drills, and insisting on their observance, that we can ensure that such accidents remain a comparative rarity. So however modest an occasion it may be, whether a day on a small rough shoot, or just a lone foray with your dog, always be as immaculate in matters of safety as you would if attending a covert shoot in the company of royalty.

I have so far dealt with points of ethics rather than the mechanics of shooting. The former provide a background to the latter of which we must never lose sight. Those opposed to field sports love to represent shooting men as blood-stained assassins engaged in the senseless slaughter of animals. The reality, we know, is very different, for those who shoot have a real affection for and interest in the creatures they pursue, and play in many instances a positive and constructive role in game and wildlife conservation, just as our forbears have done, to which history bears ample witness.

We have a good case in this respect, and when need be, we must not be afraid to advance it with all the eloquence we can command if we wish to be able to continue to enjoy our sport. But to go further into the ethics of the matter is outside the scope of this book, so let

11

us turn to the mechanics.

There is nothing new about the theory of shooting moving targets. It is simply a matter of discharging a missile so that it travels on a collision course with the target. The crux of the problem lies in finding the correct course. The obvious answer is to select a point in space ahead of the target, and discharge the missile so that it arrives at this point simultaneously with the target. But although game shots are only concerned with ranges up to 45 yds or thereabouts, it has been found very difficult, even with the benefit of much practice, to estimate the point at which to aim correctly, and to do this consistently successfully almost impossible. It was then suggested that if a gun, instead of being static when fired, was swung along the line of flight of the target and on ahead, the trigger being pulled while the gun was still in motion, it would both shorten the apparent distance ahead it was necessary to fire, and reduce the margin of possible error. This has become known as the 'swing and intercept' method of shooting. Although it is an obvious advance on the basic intercept technique, it still has three major drawbacks. The shooter has to divert his attention from the target in order to estimate the point in space at which to shoot, which will clearly vary from shot to shot according to the speed and angle of approach or departure of the quarry, while when a target is on the wing height will be a third dimension to be evaluated. His point of aim is unmarked. He has to transfer his eyes from the target to this vague point of aim just at the critical moment when he is about to fire.

Direct comparisons between rifle- and shotgun-shooting are often misleading because like is not being compared with like. However I believe both have this in common, that a clearly recognisable aiming-mark is essential to successful shooting; indeterminate points in space fail by definition to meet this requirement. A cardinal rule in all games such as golf, cricket, or squash is to keep your eye on the ball until you have completed your shot; leading players all agree that anything which even momentarily distracts the eye as the ball is about to be struck is liable to cause a mishit. So it seems to me that any method that requires the shooter both to divert his attention to a mental calculation and to take his eye off the 'ball' at this critical juncture, must be fundamentally unsound.

To the best of my belief it was the late Robert Churchill who first put forward the idea that it was just as necessary for the game shot to keep his eye on the 'ball' as the golfer or cricketer, and proclaimed the theory of 'Overthrow' which enabled this to be done. How this theory operates and is applied in practice will be explained later. Suffice it to say that it enables the shooter to rely on the instinctive coordination of hand and eye to shoot apparently straight at a moving target and hit it. It also disposes of the three objections to the swing and intercept method. It seems to me therefore such an overwhelmingly simpler and better method of shooting that I do not propose to refer again to the swing and intercept method,

12

nor to produce Tables showing the lead which ought to be given to targets travelling at different heights and speeds. These latter have probably caused more heartbreak amongst novice shots of all ages than almost anything which has been written about how to shoot.

A cricketer would think it stupid to turn out for a match at the beginning of a season without any prior practice at the nets, and players of other games would take a similar view if they wished to do justice to their own capabilities. Yet many a man will happily appear at his first covert shoot of the season having never held a gun in his hands since the end of the previous January. It is hardly surprising that such people seldom do justice either to themselves or the birds at which they shoot. If a shooter wishes to be in form at the beginning of a season, preliminary practice is just as necessary as for the cricketer or golfer, and although he may not have an obligation to a team to consider, he has instead one to the quarry he goes to shoot, which should weigh no less. Shooting schools may not always be within easy reach for a 'round with the pro' so to speak. But with a little initiative some sort of useful practice at clays can nearly always be arranged locally — an elaborate layout is not necessary; great fun can be had with just one trap if it is skilfully sited, or even only a hand-thrower. If you are paying a substantial price for a gun for a season in a syndicate, it seems foolish to quibble at the expenditure of only a few pounds more to obtain the practice which will enable you to shoot your best, and so gain that extra enjoyment which satisfactory performance gives.

Earlier I have mentioned the desirability of knowing something about your gun and cartridge, and how they function. An elementary knowledge of these matters is a genuine asset to a sportsman. The next chapter is devoted to this subject, and I commend it to all readers. I am well aware of the antipathy, especially of many older sportsmen, to anything 'technical', but in my experience this is more often a pose than inability to assimilate simple facts which could be of material assistance in obtaining good results. For example, many young shots find when they start shooting with a .410 that they only wound creatures instead of killing them cleanly; the common remedy is to give them cartridges loaded with larger shot. This merely aggravates the condition it is intended to cure, because the fault with these small guns is the lack of pellets in the charge, not inadequate striking energy. The reasons why this is so are not hard to grasp, as is the case with many other simple matters of which it would be helpful to know.

In fact the aura of mystery with which guns and cartridges have become surrounded is almost entirely unwarranted.

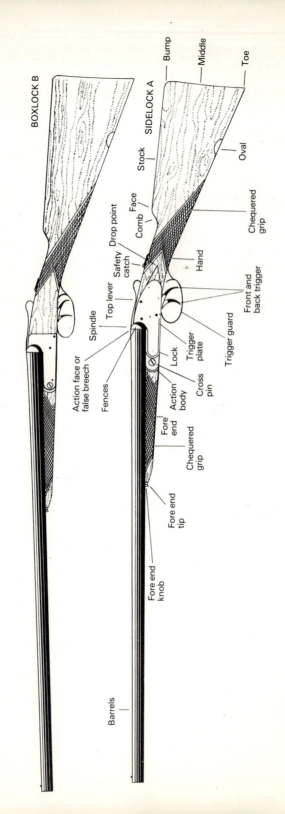

1. The Parts of a Hammerless Ejector Game Gun: (a) A Sidelock, (b) A Boxlock.

2 practical gun know-how

Shotguns — their Gauges and Weights

The parts of a typical hammerless ejector game gun are shown in *Diagram 1*. It will be seen that they are essentially the same for the sidelock, depicted at 1a, and the boxlock, at 1b. Hammer guns are still made in small numbers by some overseas makers, and secondhand examples of British make are obtainable. But although some fine specimens of the latter can sometimes be found, it is the hammerless gun with which the modern shooter is really concerned.

Early firearms shot a lead ball, and were graded according to its size. Thus a cannon firing a 2-lb. lead sphere was defined as a two-pounder, and so on. When hand guns made their appearance, the system had to be modified, because the weight of the projectile they handled was less than 1 lb. They were classified instead by the number of lead spheres, each exactly fitting the bore, which went to make up 1 lb. So if 16 such spheres went to the pound, the weapon was a 16-bore, and if the number was 12, it was a 12-bore, and so on. The first shotguns were graded in the same way, and because the bore sizes in general use have remained much the same, unlike those for weapons handling ball ammunition, the nomenclature has been retained. The only exception is the .410, which was introduced at a much later date when it had become current practice to differentiate firearms by the diameter of the bore. The bore sizes in general use to-day are given *in Table 1*.

Table 1

Gauge	Diameter of Bore in Inches
4	.938
8	.835
10	.775
12	.729
16	.662
20	.615
28	.550
.410	.410

Guns of other gauges, e.g. 14-bore and 24-bore, have been made but are extremely rare, and ammunition for them has not been produced in Britain for many years.

For game shooting in the British Isles it has long since become widely recognised that the 12-bore offers the best combination of weight and performance. However some sportsmen prefer the lighter 16-bore or 20-bore, while young shots generally start with a 28-bore or .410. *Table 2* shows the weights to which guns of different gauges, and handling varying loads, are normally made; the chamber-lengths in inches are shown in brackets.

Table 2

Gun Gauge	*Shot Charge in Ozs*	*Gun Weight in Lbs*
4 (4 in.)	3 — 4	$14\frac{1}{2}$ — 19
8 ($3\frac{1}{4}$ in.)	2 — $2\frac{1}{2}$	$10\frac{1}{2}$ — 13
10 ($2\frac{7}{8}$ in.)	$1\frac{7}{16}$	8 — 9
10 ($2\frac{5}{8}$ in.)	$1\frac{5}{16}$	$7\frac{1}{2}$ — 8
12 (3 in.)	$1\frac{1}{2}$ — $1\frac{5}{8}$	$8\frac{1}{4}$ — 9
12 ($2\frac{3}{4}$ in.)	$1\frac{1}{4}$ — $1\frac{1}{2}$	7 — $8\frac{1}{4}$
12 ($2\frac{1}{2}$ in.)	1 — $1\frac{1}{8}$*	6 — $6\frac{3}{4}$
12 (2 in.)	$\frac{7}{8}$	$5\frac{1}{4}$ — $5\frac{3}{4}$
16 ($2\frac{3}{4}$ in.)	$1\frac{1}{8}$	$6\frac{1}{2}$ — $6\frac{3}{4}$
16 ($2\frac{1}{2}$ in.)	$\frac{15}{16}$	$5\frac{1}{2}$ — 6
20 ($2\frac{3}{4}$ in.)	1	6 — $6\frac{1}{4}$
20 ($2\frac{1}{2}$ in.)	$\frac{13}{16}$	$5\frac{1}{4}$ — $5\frac{1}{2}$
28 ($2\frac{1}{2}$ in.)	$\frac{9}{16}$	$4\frac{3}{4}$ — $5\frac{1}{4}$
.410 (3 in.)	$\frac{5}{8}$	5 — $5\frac{1}{4}$
.410 ($2\frac{1}{2}$ in.)	$\frac{7}{16}$	4 — $4\frac{3}{4}$
.410 (2 in.)	$\frac{5}{16}$	$3\frac{3}{4}$ — 4

* *Note.* The 12-bore standard load is $1\frac{1}{16}$ oz., and is consequently the most generally used. The Eley 'Maximum' $1\frac{3}{16}$ oz. load has been specially devised for use in the $2\frac{1}{2}$-in. chambered 12-bore.

Guns in these various categories of slightly different weights may be found, probably lighter rather than heavier than those shown. The disadvantages of very light guns are explained in Part II of this Chapter, and it is considered advisable to stick to the weights given.

Guns New and Secondhand

Prices of guns vary enormously. In 1978 a new, best, London-made, hammerless, sidelock, easy-opening ejector would have cost around £6,500, a first-quality British boxlock ejector about £2,500, a plain British boxlock ejector some £800, and a plain boxlock of reputable foreign make approximately £240. Sound secondhand guns in these various grades can be acquired for somewhat less.

In view of the high prices of good quality new guns and secondhand ones which have been thoroughly renovated, some people prefer to try and find a 'bargain' on their own account. It is still perfectly possible to do this, but it is advisable to know the points of difference between a genuinely good, old gun, and one that merely appears to fit this description. Probably the first thing a prospective buyer will look at is the maker's name. It is very nice to own a gun carrying the name of a leading maker such as Purdey, Holland & Holland, Boss, Woodward, Grant, Lang, Dickson, etc, and it is quite rightly regarded as a mark of quality. However, many things can happen to a gun in the interval between its original sale by the maker and its appearance, possibly many years later, for sale secondhand. It may have been inexpensively rebarrelled by another firm, or cheaply restocked, to name but two possibilities, and such alterations or repairs will reduce the value it would otherwise have had. So I recommend anyone who buys a gun privately to do so subject to his obtaining a favourable report from either the original maker, or if this is not possible, at least a reputable gunsmith.

There may be circumstances in which a check of this kind cannot be arranged, such as when buying a gun at an auction, and the buyer finds himself having to rely entirely on his own resources. There are a number of points which can be of help in this contingency.

The Barrels

The barrels of modern shotguns are made of steel. Damascus barrels — i.e. those of steel and iron twisted and welded together — are obsolete, but secondhand guns with such barrels are still in use. They are easily recognisable by the distinctive scroll pattern of the metal, and by their being 'browned' instead of 'blued' like steel barrels. But in view of the difficulty and expense of getting Damascus barrels rebrowned nowadays, instances may be found where they have been blued, which hides the scroll pattern. The barrels of old secondhand guns which appear to have been recently blued should therefore be carefully examined to determine whether they are steel or Damascus. Even the best Damascus barrels were liable to have flaws in them, and section for section had to be made heavier than steel ones to be of equivalent strength. So I would not recommend the purchase of a gun with such barrels, unless some other factor was overwhelmingly in its favour.

If a gun has been rebarrelled other than by the original maker the name of the firm concerned has now, by law, to be shown. However if the work was done prior to this being a legal requirement, it is not always easy to detect. Best guns may sometimes have been fitted with new barrels of poorer quality than the originals, in which case they will almost certainly not be of chopper lump construction (see below), and the fences may have been slightly modified to fit flush with the new breech, in which case they will have had to be re-engraved, and this may not match up with the original engraving.

How Barrels are Joined

The barrels of double-barrelled guns are brazed together in one of

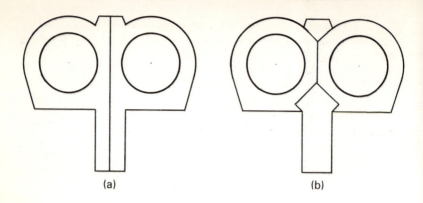

(a)   (b)

2. How the Barrels are joined at the Breech by:
(a) The Chopper Lump Method. (b) Dovetailing.
Chopper Lumps are one of the marks of a Best gun, but well
executed Dovetailing is entirely reliable.

several ways at the breech end. The two most commonly used are
the chopper lump method shown in *Diagram 2a*, and that of
dovetailing as in *Diagram 2b*. If the extractors are removed, as
described later, the tell-tale lines of the brazing will indicate quite
clearly which method has been employed. Chopper lumps give the
stronger join, but are the more costly owing to the extra metal
required to form the 'chopper' out of which the lumps are subsequently cut *(see Diagram 3)*. But the advances in fluxes and
brazing techniques since the mid-1950s have made the advantage
in strength of chopper lumps of less practical consequence, and
where the design and workmanship of dovetailing are sound it can
be entirely relied upon. However chopper lumps remain a
distinguishing feature of a best gun, though others may also have
them, notably all models in the A.Y.A. range of Spanish guns
marketed in Britain.

One further method warrants a mention, and that is the
'monobloc', as it is known. In this the whole of the breech end of the
barrels, including the flats and lumps, is machined from a single
forging, and then the actual barrels are added in a similar manner
to that in which new 'sleeved' barrels are fitted. This method is
being increasingly employed by makers overseas in the production
of modestly priced guns.

Other Parts of the Barrels

Diagram 3 shows the parts of the barrels not already depicted in
Diagram 1. The loop holds the fore-end in place, and may be either
brazed or soldered in position. It may be simply secured to the un-
derside of the barrels, or incorporate a shaped extension rising to
midway between them or a little further. Some best guns have the
loop brazed, others do not. When brazing has been employed, it is
usually quite easy to distinguish at a glance, and in my opinion is

the sounder method, especially where there is also an extension between the barrels. In cheaper, lesser quality guns the loop is almost always soldered.

The Ribs

The top and bottom ribs of the barrels are soldered in place, and in all good guns the barrel-walls enclosed between them are 'tinned', i.e. given a thin coating of solder, to deter corrosion. Even the most carefully fastened ribs may suffer from subsequent neglect, so a thorough inspection should be made of their join with the barrels on a secondhand gun to see that it is flawless. If, when the barrels are shaken close to the ear, debris can be heard rattling about in the tunnel between the ribs, it will indicate that pieces of solder have come adrift and the likelihood of corrosion having set in. If this has been going on for some years unchecked it may mean that the strength of the barrel-walls has been seriously impaired, and the only remedy is new barrels. To find out precisely how little or great the damage is, it is necessary to strip the ribs. So unless a gun was immaculate in every other respect, I would avoid buying one giving any indication of trouble of this kind.

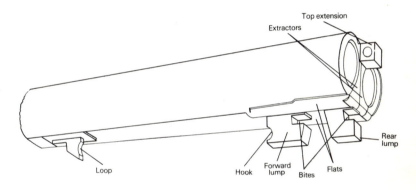

3. Parts of the Barrels

Some foreign guns have the ribs brazed. It is claimed that this makes a stronger join, but I do not believe there is any merit in this.

There are different types of top rib, as illustrated in *Diagram 4*. Which serves best is very much a matter of individual taste. Some practical considerations which might affect a choice are discussed in Chapter 8.

Dents and Bulges

The most common cause of dented barrels is plain carelessness in standing a gun where people or dogs are liable to knock it over. However, a mishap resulting in a dented barrel can occur to even the most careful shooter, so the presence of one small dent in a pair

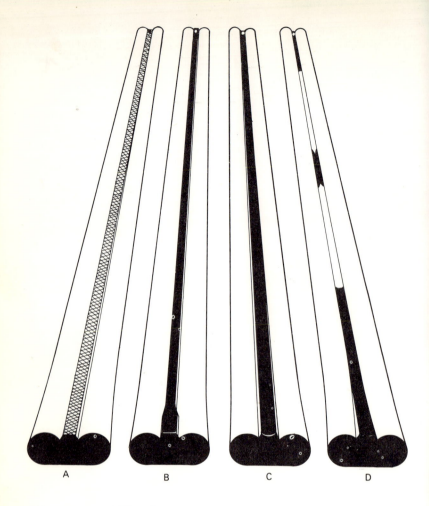

4. Three Types of Top Rib, and a Ribless Gun.
(a) A raised, flat, file-cut rib.
(b) The Churchill Tapered, Quick-sighting rib.
(c) A standard concave game rib.
(d) A pair of Alex Martin ribless barrels.

of barrels need not be cause for undue concern. But the presence of several should lead one to suspect that a gun has not been as well looked after by its previous owner as it might have been.

Dents can be detected by holding the barrels up to the light so that a line of shadow runs the length of the outside from muzzle to breech, or vice versa. If they are then slowly rotated, any irregularity that appears in this line of shadow will indicate a dent or bulge. Even a very small dent can be detected in this way, and once located is usually readily enough confirmed by eye or touch. It is also possible to pick out dents by examining the bores in the same way, but finding the corresponding flaw on the outside of the barrel is not always so easy.

The majority of dents can be raised and made good by a competent gunsmith without difficulty. Although a slightly dented barrel can usually be safely fired, it is advisable to have the dent eliminated as soon as practicable because the pimple of metal intruding into the bore is subject to greater wear than the rest of the surface every time a shot is fired, and if left untended for too long may develop into a weak point in the barrel-wall.

Some gunsmiths raise dents with the help of an instrument which they expand in the bore. If this is used too enthusiastically it can cause a ring bulge, and I have seen one or two guns to which this has probably happened; it is not easy to make good such damage.

If a pair of barrels are suspended by the hook of the forward lump, and then lightly tapped with a piece of wood, they should give a true ring. If they do not it will mean there is a flaw in them, and the gun in question should be left well alone.

The Bores

The bores should be free of pitting and corrosion. The surfaces just in front of the chamber and behind the choke should be specially checked for signs of these. Slight pitting can be lapped out readily enough without unduly enlarging the bore. However pitting is sometimes removed in this way before a gun is offered for sale, and if it was at all deep the bore may have been enlarged to the limit permitted by proof. It is illegal to sell guns that are out of proof (see end of Part III of Chapter), so an auctioneer should have gauged all weapons offered for sale to make certain the bores are within prescribed limits. A potential buyer should therefore be able to obtain relevant information on the state of the bores of any gun in which he is interested. The nominal bore-sizes, which are taken at a point 9 in. from the breech-face, have been given in Table 1. Some makers used to bore their barrels a little on the full side — say, in the case of a 12-bore, .732 in. instead of .729. So a pair of barrels gauging .735 or .736, and bearing the name of a reputable maker, should still be satisfactory but I would have reservations about barrels that gauged any larger.

Choke

The purpose of choke in a gun is to concentrate the shot charge, because it was found that with true cylinder borings patterns beyond 35 yds became too thin and erratic in quality to be properly effective. Choke is normally constructed as shown in *Diagram 5*. From this it will be seen that it consists of a cone leading into a parallel which ends at the muzzle. In principle the greater the degree of choke, the longer the cone and corresponding parallel. The usual limits within which these are made are indicated on the diagram. The nominal constrictions used for standard choke borings are given in *Table 3*.

Table 3

BORE OF GUN	CONSTRICTION IN THOUSANDTHS OF AN INCH				
	IMP CYL	$\frac{1}{4}$ CHOKE	$\frac{1}{2}$ CHOKE	$\frac{3}{4}$ CHOKE	FULL CHOKE
.410	3	6	12	16	24
28	3	7	14	21	30
20	3 — 5	8	16	24	34
16	3 — 5	9	18	26	37
12	3 — 5	10	20	30	40
10	5	11	22	32	43

(*Note* Comparable increases occur in still larger bores.)

The percentages of the total shot charge which these constrictions should place in a 30-in. circle at 40 yds, and other ranges, are given in *Table 11*.

The figures in Table 3 are not always strictly adhered to; for example, at least one gunmaker uses 8 or 9 points of choke for a 12-bore improved cylinder. Also, unless a gun has been properly regulated, it should not be assumed a barrel with a given constriction will necessarily shoot the anticipated percentage pattern. This is especially the case with foreign guns produced in quantity, of which only a sample are tested on the plate; it can likewise be so with older secondhand British guns which were originally regulated to handle rather heavier charges than are now standard. As an example of the latter, improved cylinder-barrels may quite often be found to shoot almost quarter-choke patterns. This is not a serious aberration, but where half-choke barrels are found to shoot full-choke patterns, it is, and matters should be adjusted.

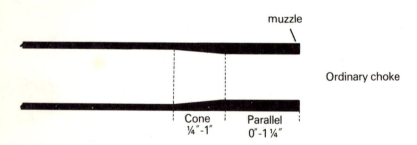

muzzle

Ordinary choke

Cone ¼"-1"   Parallel 0"-1 ¼"

5. A Cross-section of the Choke as normally built into a Barrel.

If barrels have more choke than required, it is a simple matter to have some removed, though it is work that needs to be competently executed, and you should insist on seeing and checking the patterns on the plate afterwards. It is seldom practicable to increase choke in a barrel, though by the process of recessing (see *Diagram 6*), it is sometimes possible to effect a small improvement, sufficient, say, to make a true cylinder into an improved cylinder. But in my view true cylinder barrels are better avoided.

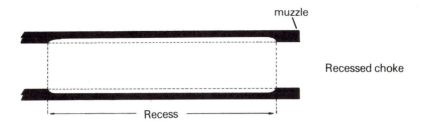

6. The Cross-section of a Recessed Choke.

Since the development of swaged chokes (see *Diagram 7*), it has become possible to restore some amount of choke to barrels which have been cut down. As will be seen, swaging consists simply in compressing the muzzle in a special machine so that the choke has a cone but no parallel. Its application is therefore limited to about a quarter-choke, if the thickness of the barrel-walls permits. However it has been found that swaged chokes shoot excellent-quality patterns, a point to be remembered in their favour when considering a gun which has been so treated.

7. The Cross-section of a Swaged Choke.

The Action

The action of a gun is the most complex and expensive part of it; it also takes the longest time to construct. It is here therefore that the majority of the distinctions between best, good, and indifferent guns are to be found.

The outside of an action can be given either a 'silver' or case-hardened finish. The latter is the more usual, and is distinguished by its attractive irregular pattern of colours, varying from dark to light blue, pale green and fawn. When a gun is new, or has been little used, this is visible in all its glory. Conversely, if only faint traces remain, it indicates that a gun has been well used.

The quality of the engraving, rather than its extent, gives a good guide to the quality of a gun, because first-class engraving is not wasted on second-class guns. When new the engraving will be much more sharply defined than after a gun has received a lot of usage.

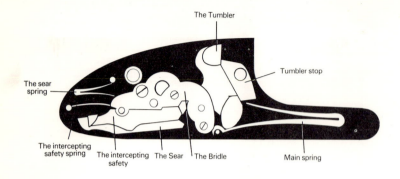

The Tumbler

Tumbler stop

The sear spring

The intercepting safety spring
The intercepting safety
The Sear
The Bridle
Main spring

8. A typical Bar Action Sidelock.

The majority of guns have either a boxlock or sidelock action. A typical bar-action sidelock is shown in *Diagram 8*. If this is looked at in conjunction with Diagram 1a, it will be seen that in an action of this type each lock is carried on a separate plate, with the main part of the mechanism fitting into a space cut out of each side of the head of the stock behind the bar of the action, in which room only has to be found for the mainspring.

An example of a modern boxlock action is illustrated in *Diagram 9*. When viewed in conjunction with Diagram 1b, it will be noted that both locks are built into the bar of the action, and have certain parts in common, notably the tumbler axle.

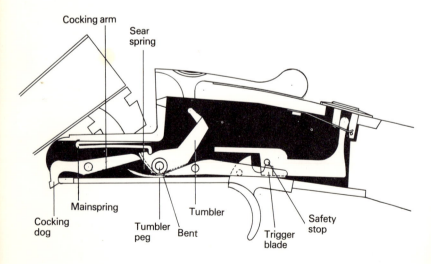

Cocking arm
Sear spring

Mainspring
Cocking dog
Tumbler peg
Bent
Tumbler
Trigger blade
Safety stop

9. The Webley & Scott 'Anson & Deeley' Boxlock Action.

Comparative Merits of Sidelock and Boxlock

Because only the mainspring of a bar-action sidelock has to be accommodated in the bar of the action, it is possible to make the cross-section of the bar stronger than that of a boxlock. Also, because of the limitations on space in a boxlock, it is possible to site the working parts of a sidelock to better mechanical advantage, and a more massive mainspring can be employed.

Again due to the advantage of greater space, a good sidelock is almost invariably equipped with an intercepting safety device, while a boxlock isn't. In this connection, it should be noted that the safety-catch on a gun only locks the triggers when applied (see Diagram 9). Thus if a gun is jarred it is possible for the nose of the sear to come out of the bent, so allowing the tumbler to be impelled forward by the mainspring and, if the gun is loaded, fire the cartridge. If such a mishap occurs, an intercepting safety is designed to catch the tumbler as it falls in a sort of half-cock position. Although in a good quality, properly adjusted lock, an exceptionally severe jolt would be needed to cause the sear nose to jump out of the bent, the advantage of having an intercepting safety incorporated is undeniable. The best of these devices are as near foolproof as human ingenuity can make them, but anything mechanical is fallible and rare instances have been known of them failing. So a gun thus equipped should be handled with no less regard for safety drills than one that isn't.

Most best sidelock guns are equipped with a self-opening or easy-opening mechanism, whereas only one make of top-quality boxlock is, namely, the Churchill 'Hercules', and this is yet again principally a question of available space. There is no disputing the advantage of such a mechanism, but I would consider it a bonus rather than an essential.

From the above it will be realised that a sidelock action is stronger, more mechanically efficient, and if an intercepting safety is incorporated, safer than a boxlock. But these advantages must be weighed in terms of their practical relevance. Since Messrs Anson & Deeley introduced their boxlock design in 1875 it has remained basically unchanged, and is still the most widely used in modern gunmaking throughout the world. It has the virtue of simplicity, so that boxlocks are easier and cheaper to make. Had there been any really fundamental weakness in the respects mentioned, it could not have survived so well and long in use. A first-quality boxlock will stand up to normal hard usage in the shooting field just as well as an equivalent sidelock, but it will not so well withstand abuse. I must stress the importance of good quality steel and sound workmanship in the making of boxlocks. If either of these is deficient, a boxlock can become genuinely unsafe, and for this reason one can but be suspicious of very cheap foreign guns of this type.

The Fastening of Barrels to Action

An important part of the action is the mechanism for securing the barrels when the breech is closed. *Diagram 10* shows how this is achieved by the Purdey Double-Bolt, usually actuated by a top lever, **F**, though a side or under lever may be employed instead. As will be seen, this bolt has two tongues, **B** and **C**, which fit into the bites in the lumps of the barrels, **D** and **E**, respectively. Bolt **B** in the forward lump acts more in the nature of a guide; it is bolt **C** that must fit really tightly down on bite **E** in the rear lump to give a secure closure. If this is as snug a fit as it ought to be, the maximum acceptable pressure will be needed to operate the top lever, **F** in order to open the breech. In some guns a top extension is fitted in the region of point **G** in order to reinforce bolt **C**. But if a crossbolt at **G** is to play a useful part, it should fit no less closely than bolt **C**. However if we make this so, excessive pressure will be needed to work the top lever, and we can only restore this to what is acceptable by relaxing the fit of bolt **C** to compensate for that we have added at **G**. There is no advantage in this, and it is simply using two bolts to do the work of one. I hope this illustrates the futility of top extensions, quite apart from them being an obstacle to quick reloading, and a source of bruised fingers when cleaning a gun.

When the Purdey double-bolt is withdrawn, the barrels will rotate about the crosspin, **A**. In a best gun this will be an actual pin inserted across the knuckle of the action, and held in place by a small plate screwed home on each side of the knuckle, one of which may be fashioned to resemble a screwhead. In the majority of guns other than best, the crosspin is cut out of the steel of the knuckle, and although there may be a dummy screwhead at one side of the knuckle, it will not be removable.

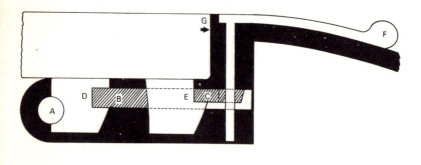

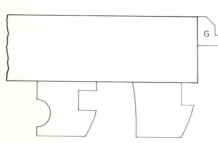

10. The Purdey Double-Bolt Closure. The bolt is shown at 'B' and 'C' fitted into the bites of the Lumps at 'D' and 'E' respectively. In some guns a Top Extension, 'G', is incorporated to reinforce the fastening provided by the double-bolt; but see text.

The breech of the barrels should fit tight on to the face of the action, and the flats of the barrels be flush with those of the action. If a gun is held sideways up to the light, any gap which has developed between the breech and the face should be clearly revealed, or in other words the barrels will have 'come off the face'. Where a gun has a genuine crosspin, a gunsmith can easily remedy this by replacing it with a larger one. But if a gun has a solid knuckle the situation is not so easily restored. If therefore you find the barrels of a gun are quite noticeably off the face, and it appears to have a solid knuckle, it is probably wiser to seek another gun.

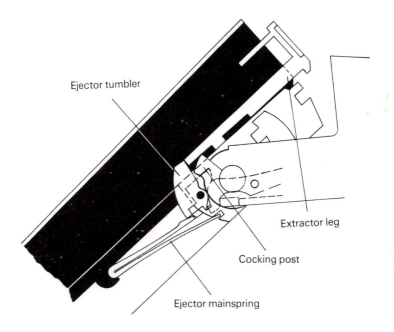

Ejector tumbler

Extractor leg

Cocking post

Ejector mainspring

11. The Southgate Ejector Mechanism.

The Ejectors

An efficient ejector system is an invaluable aid to quick shooting, especially when tackling driven game. The one most commonly used in British guns for many years has been the Southgate (see *Diagram 11*). This is built into the fore-end, and comprises two miniature locks. Each tumbler, or kicker, is actuated by a V-spring, and is released as it goes 'over-centre', like the blade of a penknife, causing it to strike its opposing extractor-leg a smart blow. This is timed so that the breech will have opened sufficiently to allow the empty cartridge-case to be thrown clear of the top of the action face. The kicker is recocked as the gun is closed. Many gunmakers have developed their own variations of the Southgate system.

The Triggers

Trigger-pulls are normally adjusted so that that of the front trigger is $3\frac{1}{2}$ — 4lb, and that of the rear one 4 — $4\frac{1}{2}$ lb., on account of the greater leverage obtained on the latter. A sidelock allows of rather finer adjustment than a boxlock, though unless one is very sensitive in this respect, the latter will permit as 'crisp' a pull as most shooters require. With cheap boxlocks the poor quality of the steel of sears and bents may make good adjustment of the trigger-pulls almost impossible, without incurring the danger of the locks jarring off accidentally.

In secondhand guns the trigger-pulls may be found sometimes to be rather sluggish due to old oil having congealed and clogged the working parts, but this is easily cured. When testing trigger-pulls, snap caps — i.e. dummy rounds — should always be inserted in the chambers.

Some people prefer single triggers. There are two basic types, the selective and the non-selective, the former allowing the left barrel to be fired first by manipulating a change lever, which may be either a small slide on the side of the action, or incorporated in the safety catch; selective mechanisms are the more predominant. From my own experience I have not found any practical advantage in a single trigger over conventional double triggers. I believe therefore it is a matter in which one should follow one's fancy, and anyone who imagines he shoots better with a single trigger should have one.

Other Actions and Guns

The Dickson 'Round Action' is quite distinctive from both boxlock and sidelock, and is depicted in *Diagram 12*. Both locks are built up on a vertical central plate which is mounted on the trigger-plate, and the ejector system is built into the body of the action. This is a most admirable action, in all respects on a par with a best sidelock. If you live outside Scotland, there is one possible snag in owning such a gun: not all gunsmiths really understand this action and are competent to effect repairs.

Some game shots prefer an 'over and under' to the more usual side-by-side. I have only a small experience of shooting with an over and under, but I believe the hazard of canting the barrels when turning to take a shot is considerably aggravated, and this is of course a well recognised cause of missing. They are more expensive owing to the greater intricacy of the design and wider drop that has to be given to the barrels to enable the spent case to be ejected from the bottom chamber. Also, unless a lighter alloy is used for the action body, the extra steel required means that they have to be built about $\frac{1}{4}$-lb. heavier than an equivalent side-by-side gun.

On grounds of safety I have serious reservations about the suitability of automatic and repeating shotguns for game shooting. Unloading and reloading when crossing fences, and on other appropriate occasions in the shooting field, is trickier and more time-

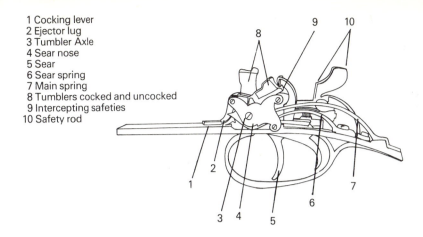

1 Cocking lever
2 Ejector lug
3 Tumbler Axle
4 Sear nose
5 Sear
6 Sear spring
7 Main spring
8 Tumblers cocked and uncocked
9 Intercepting safeties
10 Safety rod

12. The Dickson 'Round Action'.
This admirable action offers a unique combination of strength and mechanical efficiency.

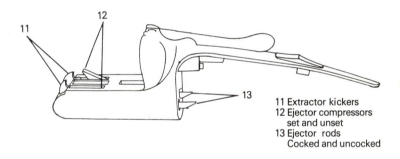

11 Extractor kickers
12 Ejector compressors
   set and unset
13 Ejector rods
   Cocked and uncocked

consuming. Also these weapons cannot be seen at a glance to be loaded or unloaded. To check whether or not the barrel is free of obstruction before loading it has to be inspected from the muzzle. They have a further disadvantage; owing to parts of the mechanism which are built into the stock, it is not feasible to have alterations made to bend and cast off.

The Stock and Fore-end
The stocks of all reputable guns are made from walnut, and the better the quality of the gun the better that of the timber used. British game-guns usually have a straight hand-stock, as illustrated in *Diagram 13a*. Quarter pistol-grips, half pistol-grips and full pistol-grips, as shown in *Diagrams 13b, c,* and *d,* are comparatively rare other than in conjunction with a single trigger. The 'Monte Carlo' type stock in Diagram 13d is used to provide a high cheek-piece at

the comb for those with a long neck.

The inadequacy of the traditional shaped fore-end on a game-gun in providing a good hand-hold, especially when the barrels grow warm, is well recognised. The American beaver-tail fore-end overcomes this handicap, but gives a gun a heavy, unsightly appearance. A better answer in my view is an ordinary leather-covered handguard fitted with a special clip fastening to the fore-end knob.

When buying a secondhand gun the well-worn state of the chequering may indicate that it has seen a lot of service. However it is simple and not expensive to have worn chequering on the stock and fore-end recut, so this is by no means an infallible guide to age, or amount of usage.

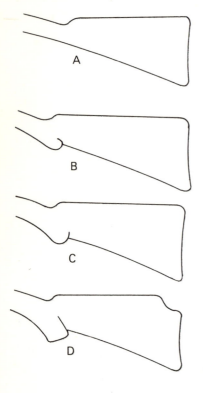

13. Four types of Stock.
(a) A Straight Hand Stock.
(b) A Quarter Pistol Grip.
(c) A Half Pistol Grip.
(d) A 'Monte Carlo' type stock with a full Pistol Grip and raised cheekpiece.

PART II — THE CARTRIDGE

General

A section of a modern British cartridge, illustrating its various components, is shown in *Diagram 14*. All propellants used in such cartridges are smokeless and designed to give satisfactory and consistent ballistics, as well as to retain their stability in spite of rough handling and varying climatic conditions. All caps nowadays contain a non-corrosive detonating compound, and are carefully matched to the propellant to ensure its complete and instantaneous combustion. The case is made of either lacquered paper or plastic, the former being only water-resistant, while the latter is waterproof. The lead shot is alloyed with special hardening-agents, and should be perfectly spherical and uniform in size for each shot-size. The main wad and closure may seem of comparatively minor significance, but both play a major role in ensuring good ballistics, and consequently satisfactory results in the shooting-field.

So many myths and misunderstandings about cartridges and their performance prevail amongst sportsmen that I feel it is high time an attempt was made to try to put the record straight in simple terms on certain points, although I realise many may regard this as a sort of heresy comparable to casting doubt on the credibility of the Delphic oracle in its heyday.

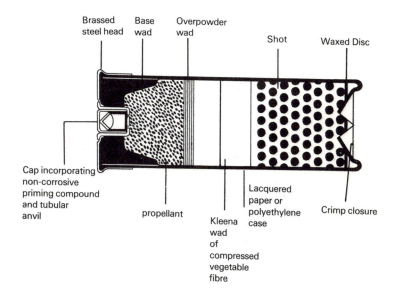

14. A Section of a Modern British Game Cartridge.

The Wad

The main wad has to seal the bore so that the gases generated by the propellant cannot escape past it as they propel the shot-charge down the bore. It must therefore be made of material which is sufficiently elastic to expand enough to serve this purpose when compressed by the gases behind against the shot-column in front. It should also be as light in weight as possible to minimise recoil. The Eley 'Kleena' wad, made of compressed vegetable fibres, fulfils these conditions admirably. Good quality felt wads are also

31

Table 4

THE NUMBER OF PELLETS IN DIFFERENT CHARGES OF SHOT

SIZE OF SHOT	1⅝	1½	1¼	1 3/16	1⅛	1 1/16	1	15/16	⅞	13/16	⅝	9/16	7/16	5/16
						OUNCES								
BB	114	105	88	83	79	74	70	—	—	—	—	—	—	—
1	163	150	125	119	113	106	100	—	—	—	—	—	—	—
3	228	210	175	166	158	149	140	—	—	—	—	—	—	—
4	276	255	213	202	191	181	170	159	149	138	—	—	—	—
5	—	—	275	261	248	234	220	206	193	179	138	124	—	—
6	—	—	—	321	304	287	270	253	236	219	169	152	118	84
7	—	—	—	—	383	361	340	319	298	276	212	191	149	106
8	—	—	—	—	506	478	450	422	394	366	281	253	196	140
9	—	—	—	—	—	616	580	544	508	471	363	326	254	184

satisfactory, but inferior quality ones much less so. Cork wads tend to give rather low and variable ballistics, because cork being a natural substance lacks uniform quality. In fact it is the lower ballistics, and hence lower recoil, induced by cork wadding rather than its lightness, that enables cartridges with cork wads to 'cure' gun headache, which is simply a form of mild concussion. The latest development is the plastic wad, which has been found to combine good obturation with extreme lightness. This latter quality allows a marginal reduction in the amount of the propellant, and hence in noticeable recoil.

The Closure

The closure of a cartridge is effected either by a crimp, or a top wad and rolled turnover. The former is preferable as it has been found to give rather better quality and more regular patterns, but is impracticable in certain instances, such as with large shot.

When a cartridge is fired the resistance of the closure has to be overcome in addition to the inertia of the shot-column by the expanding gases, before the charge starts to move down the bore. This resistance must permit a proper build-up of pressure but give way before it becomes excessive. The amount of pressure required to reach this critical point is known as the 'pull-out strength' of the closure. It will be appreciated that in order to have consistent round-to-round ballistics the pull-out strength of every cartridge-case must be exactly the same. It is therefore most important that the closure of a cartridge is well designed and fashioned. This is one of the first points I check in a new brand of cartridges, especially if they are imported.

Shot Loads

The number of pellets of various sizes in different loads is given in *Table 4*.

Pressure

The importance of pressure is in the main little appreciated. Yet satisfactory and consistent pressures mean effective, good-quality patterns, which give the best chance of success in the field. High pressures tend to disperse patterns, thus lessening the possibilities of killing cleanly; they also induce heavier recoil, making quick, accurate second-barrel shots more difficult. Weak pressures give rise to lower velocities, with consequent loss of penetration, increasing the chances of merely wounding.

The heavier a shot-load to be projected at a stipulated velocity from a barrel of given bore, the greater the pressure required. Extensive research by cartridge-makers has shown that the most satisfactory and uniform pressures are obtained when the length of a shot-load in a cartridge is the same as the width of the bore. Owing to their excellent performance these 'square loads' have almost without exception been adopted as the 'standard load' for each different gauge. The standard loads for gauges with which a game-shooter is concerned are shown in *Table 5*.

Table 5

BORE	LOAD IN OUNCES
12	$1\frac{1}{16}$
16	$\frac{15}{16}$
20	$\frac{13}{16}$
28	$\frac{9}{16}$
.410	$\frac{7}{16}$

We have probably all wondered at some time if more powder and shot might not provide the magic touch needed to transform us into crack shots. Alas, they won't. Heavier and faster loads are not intended to compensate for lack of shooting skill, but to give better penetration and pattern at long range when shooting more heavily plumaged quarry, such as wildfowl. Also, to gain full advantage from them they should be used in conjunction with well-choked barrels, not lightly-choked game-guns, which owing to the greater pressure will not hold the patterns properly together. Those who wish to give themselves the best chance of success in game-shooting cannot do better than pin their faith on the standard load, and this is as true if they are shooting with a 28-bore as a 12-bore.

Velocity

Shotgun performance is not compared in terms of muzzle-velocity as is that of rifles. This is because light pellets, like No.8's, lose their velocity more rapidly than heavier ones, such as No.3's; in order to give the former a reasonably comparable effective range in relation to pattern density, they have to be sped on their way with a higher muzzle-velocity. Thus it is true that the shooter experiences slightly more recoil with a given load of small-sized shot than with one of larger. However a satisfactory method of comparing velocities has been found in terms of the mean velocity of pellets of all sizes over the first twenty yards of their flight, which is known as the 'observed velocity'. 'Standard velocity' — i.e. of a standard load is an observed velocity of 1070 ft per second (f.p.s.), and 'high velocity' one of 1120 f.p.s. Other observed velocities of interest are that of the 'Maximum' cartridge, which is 1090 f.p.s., and of trap cartridges which is 1030 f.p.s.

The limits within which observed velocities can be successfully varied are very narrow; above 1150 f.p.s. patterning becomes extremely erratic and recoil unacceptable; below 1000 f.p.s. the penetration of small shot soon becomes inadequate.

The effect of barrel-length on velocity is sometimes queried. It has been proven that shorter barrels do give lower observed velocities than longer ones, but for practical purposes the difference, even between 25-in. and 30-in. barrels, is insignificant.

Recoil

Recoil is the rearward thrust imparted to a gun when a cartridge is fired and is measured in terms of momentum, i.e. the sum of the mass of the gun in pounds and its velocity in f.p.s. This is equal to the momentum of the ejecta, i.e. the weight of the shot + wadding + propellant in lb. × the muzzle-velocity in f.p.s.

The recoil experienced by the shooter is generally referred to as 'noticeable recoil'. This is because by using propellants which burn at different rates, recoil can be made to feel like a quick, barely perceptible stab, or a pronounced shove, though both are the same in mathematical terms. But although the makers of good cartridges always try to make recoil as unnoticeable as possible, it is advisable to keep to certain minimum gun-weights to handle different loads. It has been found in practice that a minimum gun-weight of 6 lb. is desirable to handle a 1-oz. standard velocity load; a gun of at least $6\frac{1}{4}$ lb. should be used with the full standard load of $1\frac{1}{16}$ oz., while the H.V. load of $1\frac{1}{8}$ oz. requires one of almost $6\frac{3}{4}$ lb. if a shooter is not to suffer unduly from recoil. It is of course possible to fire one or two rounds from guns lighter than these without any particular discomfort, but if a quantity of shots are fired the cumulative effects of excessive recoil will cause painful bruising of cheek and jaw accompanied by mild concussion. It is therefore a sound maxim that light guns should be used only with light loads, and that heavy loads require heavy guns. Magnums are no exception to this; for example, a 20-bore magnum needs to be the same weight as a 12-bore game-gun in order to handle a 1-oz. load as comfortably. In fact the larger bore will handle the load rather more comfortably as well as more efficiently.

Storage and Choice of Cartridges

Despite the advent of the plastic waterproof case, and the notable stability of modern propellants, it is still advisable to store cartridges at normal living-room temperature and humidity if you wish to obtain the best results from them.

Some shooting-men boast that they use the cheapest cartridges they can buy. One person with whom I used to shoot did so despite the acquisition of a new pair of best sidelock ejectors, though the incongruity of that seemed to elude him. As it happened I had recently tested some of the cartridges favoured by him, and had found them wanting in several respects, chiefly I suspected due to a poor closure. Nobody in his senses wishes to spend more on cartridges than he need, but I believe a sound, well made cartridge is worth its price, because it will ensure you obtain as good results as your standard of marksmanship allows. Failure due to our own lack of skill is quite exasperating enough without bad cartridges compounding the agony.

PART III — HAPPY MARRIAGE OF GUN AND CARTRIDGE

Lethal Patterns

The more lethal a pattern of shot, the better chance of success it gives the shooter if he places it correctly. Contrary to popular belief, competent marksmanship alone does not always suffice. Pattern can be decisive in determining whether a high bird falls dead, 'hit in the beak' as we all like to see, or a dog has to spend ten minutes finding and bringing a runner to hand.

A lethal pattern has two properties: a sufficiency of pellets to make certain that at least one finds a vital mark, and adequate striking energy in every pellet to deliver a fatal blow on that mark. We should all know how we can obtain the most advantageous patterns in both these respects in the various circumstances we are likely to encounter in the shooting field.

Pattern Density and Quality

Shotgun patterns are evaluated according to the number of pellets placed in a 30-in. circle at 40 yds range. This is because 40 yds is regarded as the limit of sporting range, and 45 yds as extreme range in game-shooting. Beyond this latter point patterns of small shot, i.e. nos. 5, 6, and 7, deteriorate very rapidly in both density and quality, though individual pellets can fly on for 200-250 yds before they become spent. But if we can be sure of a satisfactory pattern at 40 yds, we shall have nothing to worry about at closer quarters, save at the point at which it may become too dense and 'smash' the quarry at which we shoot.

Everyone is aware that a small bird like a snipe requires a denser pattern than a large one such as a cock pheasant. But there is more to assessing minimum necessary patterns than doing a simple sum involving the area of the 30-in. circle and the body-area of the creature concerned.

All the pellets in a charge do not fly true; a small percentage become so distorted during their passage up the bore and through the choke that they fly off at a tangent and are ineffective. Also, a shot-charge travels through the air as a column, not a disc, and increases in length, as in diameter, with the range. At 40 yds it is about 12 ft long, and approximately 90 per cent of the pellets are in the front 6 ft. The failing velocity of the extreme tail-enders makes their striking-energy suspect, so some allowance must be made for these as well as the 'fliers'.

Even the best regulated guns and finest cartridges do not ensure that the pellets are absolutely evenly distributed over the 30-in. circle. However the more nearly this can be achieved the better, and a good-quality pattern should have a reasonably symmetrical appearance with no glaring gaps or eye-catching clusters of pellets (see Diagram 15a). A small allowance is, however, made to offset the unavoidable irregularity in pellet distribution. The number of pellets placed in the 30-in. circle varies from round to round by as

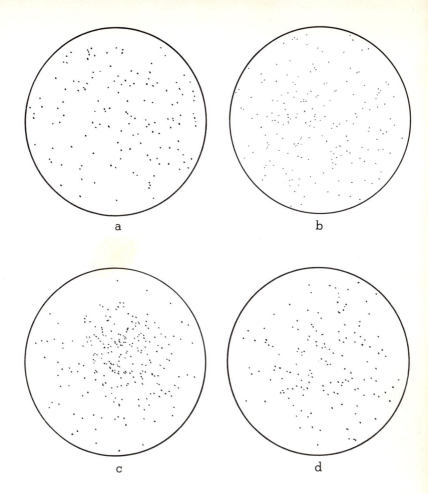

15. Four examples of Shot Patterns.
(a) A good quality improved cylinder 12-bore pattern at 40 yds using a standard load ($1\frac{1}{16}$oz.) of No.6 shot. There are 146 pellets in the 30 in. circle.
(b) A quarter-choke 12-bore pattern at 40 yds using a 1 oz. load of No.7 shot. There are 192 pellets in the 30-in. circle.
(c) An improved cylinder 12-bore pattern at 20 yds using a standard load ($1\frac{1}{16}$oz.) of No.6 shot. There are 277 pellets in the 30-in. circle, which clearly indicates the undesirability of shooting quarry at closer quarters.
(d) A good quality improved cylinder 28-bore pattern at 30 yds using a standard load ($\frac{9}{16}$oz.) of No.7 shot. There are 144 pellets in the 30-in. circle.

little as 5 per cent with a well regulated gun, to as much as 10 per cent or more with one not so well regulated.

There are also various factors to be considered concerning the quarry itself. A pheasant is obviously a heavier, stronger bird than a snipe, so it is logical to assume that even in a vital part it will need to be hit a harder blow. Further, it is clearly better armoured by flesh and bone, so that although one direct hit may suffice for a snipe, several may be necessary on a pheasant to ensure that one finds a vital mark to which it can penetrate. In other words, the larger our quarry, the smaller the proportion of its body-area that comprises a vulnerable target even though we use larger shot to strike a harder blow.

Taking all these factors into account, the estimated minimum patterns necessary for different quarry are given in *Table 6*. The estimated proportion of body-area that constitutes the actual vulnerable target-area is shown in brackets.

Table 6

Snipe	290 ($\frac{1}{2}$)
Golden Plover	220 ($\frac{1}{2}$)
Woodcock and Teal	145 ($\frac{1}{2}$)
Partridge and Woodpigeon	130 ($\frac{1}{4}$)
Grouse	120 ($\frac{1}{3}$)
Pheasant, Blackcock and Mallard	100 ($\frac{1}{5}$)
Goose and Capercaillie	70 ($\frac{1}{8}$)
Rabbit	100 ($\frac{1}{5}$)
Hare	70 ($\frac{1}{8}$)

Pellet Striking Energy

Minimum lethal striking energies of individual pellets for different quarry have been estimated largely from empiric research and experience. They are generally accepted to be as in *Table 7*.

Table 7

Very small birds: snipe, golden plover, etc.	0.50 ft lb.
Small birds: woodcock, partridge, grouse, etc.	0.85 ft lb.
Medium birds: pheasant, blackcock, mallard, etc.	1.00 ft lb.
Large Birds: capercaillie, goose, etc.	1.50 ft lb.
Rabbit	1.00 ft lb.
Hare	1.50 ft lb.

Some wildfowlers consider that 1.50 ft lb. is on the light side for a goose. But in my experience the figures in the Table hold good if pattern is of recommended density. Heavy shot will not compensate for bad marksmanship, and it is a cardinal error to use it in an attempt to do so.

The individual pellet striking energies in ft lb. of various shot-sizes at different ranges for the observed velocities concerned are given in *Tables 8, 9,* and *10*.

STRIKING ENERGIES OF INDIVIDUAL PELLETS IN FT/LBS

Table 8
OBSERVED VELOCITY 1,070 f.p.s. (Standard Velocity)

SIZE OF SHOT	RANGE IN YARDS							
	10	20	30	35	40	45	50	60
BB	15.78	12.32	9.98	8.97	8.11	7.34	6.57	5.25
1	10.61	8.46	6.62	5.88	5.25	4.65	4.11	3.18
3	7.83	5.79	4.47	3.94	3.43	2.99	2.61	1.93
4	6.43	4.66	3.52	3.04	2.65	2.28	1.96	1.42
5	4.98	3.51	2.59	2.22	1.89	1.61	1.35	0.94
6	4.94	2.79	2.01	1.71	1.43	1.21	0.99	0.66
7	3.20	2.17	1.51	1.26	1.05	0.86	0.69	0.45
8	2.40	1.57	1.06	0.86	0.70	0.56	0.45	0.27
9	1.88	1.19	0.77	0.62	0.49	0.39	0.29	0.17

Table 9
OBSERVED VELOCITY 1,120 f.p.s. (H.V.)

SIZE OF SHOT	RANGE IN YARDS							
	10	20	30	35	40	45	50	60
BB	17.23	13.32	10.68	9.62	8.71	7.94	7.04	5.70
1	11.36	9.18	7.12	6.33	5.66	5.01	4.46	3.47
3	8.53	6.23	4.81	4.26	3.71	3.25	2.84	2.11
4	7.04	5.01	3.77	3.30	2.85	2.46	2.13	1.54
5	5.43	3.77	2.77	2.38	2.04	1.73	1.47	1.02
6	4.40	2.99	2.16	1.83	1.54	1.32	1.07	0.72
7	3.48	2.31	1.62	1.36	1.13	0.93	0.75	0.49

Table 10
OBSERVED VELOCITY 1,030 f.p.s.

SIZE OF SHOT	RANGE IN YARDS							
	10	20	30	35	40	45	50	60
5	4.61	3.31	2.45	2.09	1.78	1.51	1.27	0.88
6	3.71	2.63	1.91	1.61	1.35	1.12	0.93	0.62
7	2.98	2.08	1.43	1.19	0.98	0.80	0.65	0.42
8	2.24	1.49	1.00	0.82	0.66	0.52	0.41	0.25
9	1.74	1.11	0.73	0.58	0.45	0.35	0.27	0.15

The main interest of sportsmen lies in Tables 8 and 9. But I know some who use the 1⅛-oz. trap load for shooting pheasants, and I have been asked on occasion how, apart from the extra shot, it differs from the standard load — hence Table 10. It should be noted that semi-magnum and magnum loads for wildfowl are usually high velocity, a point not always realised.

For striking energy to be properly adequate, it is generally held that it should not fall below the minimum required for about 5 yds beyond the point at which pattern-density fails. With a given load there is often the option of more pellets with adequate striking energy, or fewer with surplus striking energy. It is to the shooter's advantage to choose the former, because extra pellets can fill an otherwise crucial gap in a pattern, whereas pellets that don't are ineffective however much striking energy they possess.

Shot-sizes giving a striking energy appropriate for the quarry we wish to pursue can be selected by using Table 8 or 9 in conjunction with Table 7. To choose the best pattern-density for our purpose is slightly complex. Let us first see the effect that choke has on this. *Table 11* gives the percentage of the shot-charge placed in the 30-in. circle at various ranges by different choke borings.

Table 11

BORING OF GUN	RANGE IN YARDS								
	20	25	30	35	40	45	50	55	60
True Cyl.	90	73	60	49	40	33	27	22	18
Imp. Cyl.	96	84	72	60	50	41	33	27	22
¼ Choke.	98	89	77	65	55	46	38	30	25
½ Choke.	100	96	83	71	60	50	41	33	27
¾ Choke.	100	100	91	77	65	55	46	37	30
Full Choke.	100	100	100	84	70	59	49	40	32

A diagrammatic representation of the total spread of the shot-charge (less the 'fliers') in relation to the 30-in. circle given by an improved cylinder and full choke respectively at different ranges is shown in *Diagram 16*. Newcomers to shooting often become so engrossed with the problem of killing game at 40 yds that they overlook that of doing so at 20-30 yds, within which range bracket many of their shots will be taken. I hope Diagram 16 clearly indicates the positive advantage of the improved cylinder, its wider spread not only enhancing the chances of hitting the target, but also reducing the risk of its being smashed by too many pellets. Conversely a full choke is an undoubted handicap up to 35 yds. In principle therefore, it is beneficial to have as little choke as needful in a gun. For game-shooting in Britain it seems to me folly to have more than a half-choke in either barrel. It is common to have more choke in the left barrel than the right, but I think the advantage of this is debatable, and my own preference for general game-shooting has long been a quarter-choke in each.

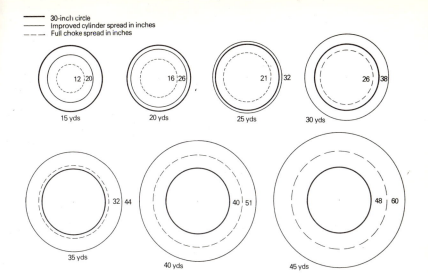

16. Diagrammatic comparison of the spread of the Shot Charge from an improved cylinder and a full choke barrel in relation to the 30-in. circle.

But returning to our pattern densities; as an example, let us consider the case of a rough-shooter with a 12-bore, the barrels of which are bored improved cylinder and half-choke, and who uses the standard-load cartridge. He will definitely want to be able to kill a pheasant or rabbit up to 40 yds, so he will need a minimum striking energy of 1 ft lb. (see Table 7) at that range. Table 8 shows that he has a choice of 7, 6, or 5 shot, though the effectiveness of No. 7 is somewhat marginal. His improved cylinder barrel gives a 50 per cent pattern at 40 yds (Table 11). Table 5 shows the number of pellets of 5, 6, and 7 shot in the standard 12-bore load as 234, 287, and 361 respectively. So the corresponding pattern-densities he can expect in the 30-in. circle at 40 yds are 117, 144, and 181. Table 6 indicates that he needs a minimum density of 100, so all these three shot-sizes will give him an effective pattern with his improved cylinder barrel at 40 yds. However at 45 yds the equivalent pattern-densities will be only 41 per cent, i.e. 96, 118, and 148 pellets respectively. Other quarry will also generally be encountered on a rough shoot, such as partridges, woodpigeon, wild duck, hares, etc. If the majority of these other creatures are likely to be smaller than a pheasant, then the advantage of greater pattern-density is obvious, and his choice of shot-size should lie between No.6 and 7. Conversely, if hares are numerous, the advantage will clearly lie with the greater striking-energy of No.5 shot. I hope this shows how simple it is to work out the most advantageous shot-size to use with a given load, and it is of course even easier if only one quarry has to be considered, such as snipe, grouse, woodpigeon, or

41

rabbits. Many myths abound regarding best shot-sizes for various quarry, but those who want to be certain on this point will be well advised to work out the answer for themselves. Always remember it is the pattern that kills, not just the striking-energy of individual pellets. Where guns of gauges smaller than 12-bore are concerned this is particularly relevant. For practical purposes the spread of the shot-charge of a 28-bore is the same as that of a 12-bore, choke for choke. So with the smaller gauges it is essential to compensate for the lighter shot-load by using a smaller shot-size in order to maintain pattern-density, and if necessary accept that this means a reduction in maximum effective range. Some specimen patterns illustrating these points are shown in *Diagrams 15a, b, c, and d.*

Gun Care and Maintenance

A shotgun is a valuable weapon, and if it is to keep its value must be properly cared for after firing and when stored away at the end of a season. Modern cleaner/lubricants in aerosol packs have taken all the hard work out of post-shooting cleaning. First the gun should be taken down into its three principal components by removing the fore-end, and then opening the breech and unhitching the barrels from the crosspin. An old plain, wooden-topped kitchen table on which to place them is ideal, as any oil spilt on it will not matter, and the surface can easily be wiped clean of debris which might otherwise scratch the stock or barrels. The cleaner/lubricant should be sprayed down the fired barrels from the breech end. The barrels should then be left flat on the table for about ten minutes. The stock and fore-end can now be wiped over with a dry cloth, and any mud in the chequering brushed out with an old toothbrush. After shooting in the rain, a piece of old flannel-shirting will serve admirably to remove the worst of the moisture, a task which I like to do as I am dismantling the gun; this should then be finished with a clean dry cloth, particular attention being paid to the knuckle and other parts of the action body into which water may have seeped. The channels on either side of the top rib should, after being wiped with a cloth, have the edge of a piece of blotting paper run down them to remove any residual damp. After the stock and fore-end have been cleaned and dried, the metal parts should be wiped over with an oily rag and just a touch of '3-in-One', or some similar penetrating oil, applied to the working parts, such as the Purdey double-bolt, the top lever, etc; the tip of a pigeon's wing feather, dipped lightly in oil, is ideal for this and for searching out the nooks and crannies, which the oily rag can't. Turning again to the barrels; I usually pull them through with a bristle brush behind which is a wad of 4 × 2 flannelette sufficiently bulky to fit the bore reasonably tightly. After each barrel has been pulled through twice, the bores should be inspected, and if there is no sign of fouling (which shows up as white streaks, especially just in front of the chamber and in the rear of the cone of the choke) the barrels can be oiled up with a wool mop not too heavily impregnated with the cleaner/lubricant. If

42

however the inspection of the bores reveals the tell-tale white streaks of leading they will have to be scrubbed out with a phosphor-bronze brush to which the cleaner/lubricant has been liberally applied. These brushes will not damage the bore and so can be used as vigorously as necessary to remove the fouling. When this has been achieved, the bores should be wiped clean, using a wool mop covered with a piece of 4×2, which can be thrown away after use. They can then be oiled up as already described.

If after shooting in the rain water is seen to have got behind the extractors, these can easily be removed by unscrewing the stop-pin in the forward lump. But it is important to use a screwdriver which fits so that you do not burr the head of the screw. After removing the extractors and wiping them dry, the tunnels in which they fit must also be dried, and for this purpose a pipe-cleaner serves well. With the aid of the pigeon-wing feather again, these tunnels can then be lightly oiled, the extractors wiped over with an oily rag and replaced, and the stop-pin restored.

There are several ways in which the wood of the stock and fore-end can be treated to keep it in good order. I find that buffing in a little boiled linseed oil with the heel of the hand is the best. But for those who may think this a trifle old-fashioned and messy, a good wax furniture polish is an excellent alternative, as is also rubbing with a silicone-impregnated cloth.

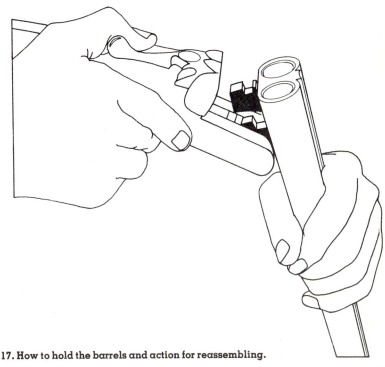

17. How to hold the barrels and action for reassembling.

When all this has been done, the gun should either be reassembled and placed in a rack or gun cabinet, or the fore-end replaced on the barrels, and these together with the stock returned to their gun case. If a gun is stiff to reassemble, as some ejectors can be, it is easy to scar the lumps or flats in the course of doing so. To avoid any such mishap, the stock should be held at the small of the butt with the right hand, the butt being held against the body by the right forearm, and the top lever being pushed over by the right thumb. The barrels should be held by the left hand close up to the breech, and the hook of the forward lump placed over the crosspin, *see Diagram 17*. If a steady pull is maintained against the crosspin as the breech is closed, there should be no trouble in effecting this smoothly. If trouble is experienced, it will usually be because the hook has not been placed properly over the crosspin in the first place; some guns are trickier than others to manipulate successfully in this way, but the knack will soon be mastered with practice.

Even though a gun may be immaculately looked after by its owner, and to the best of his knowledge suffer no damage in the course of a season, it is still sound policy to have it overhauled annually by a qualified gunsmith. Some people may consider this a waste of money, but I believe it to be good housekeeping, because unbeknown to its owner, things can go wrong with a gun which if not put right promptly can lead to complications, resulting in due course in a needlessly large repair bill.

Proof

In the early days of firearms gun barrels were frequently of such dubious quality, and the loading of charges so haphazard, that bursts were a common occurrence and often fatal. To rectify this state of affairs first the Worshipful Company of Gunmakers in London, and subsequently the Guardians of the Birmingham Proof House, established the London and Birmingham Proof Houses respectively, where gun-barrels could be properly tested. Now by Act of Parliament all guns and other firearms have to 'pass proof', as it is known, before they can legally be offered for sale. It is an offence to sell, offer for sale, exchange, or pawn any gun in Britain

(a)　　　　　　　　　　　　　　　　　　(b)

London Proof House
Provisional Proof Mark
English Make

Birmingham Proof House
Provisional Proof Mark
English Make

18. Provisional Proof Marks of:
(a) The London Proof House.
(b) The Birmingham Proof House.

(a)

12

NITRO PROOF 1⅛

(a) *Full Proof Marks, 1925–54*
London

(b)

12

NITRO PROOF 1⅛oz.

(b) *Full Proof Marks, 1925–54*
Birmingham

19. Examples of British Proof Marks in force 1925-1954 of:
(a) The London Proof House.
(b) The Birmingham Proof House.

the barrels of which have not passed proof, or are out of proof. Proof marks show only that a gun has at one time passed proof; they are not a warranty that it is still in proof. So if any doubt arises with a secondhand gun, it is advisable to have a check made by a reputable gunsmith.

The Proof Marks are impressed on the flats of the barrels. The first such mark is one indicating the passing of Provisional Proof; the relevant ones for the London and Birmingham Proof Houses are shown in *Diagrams 18a and b* respectively. Then at a later stage the gun, with the action fitted to the barrels, is sent for a further test, and another set of marks impressed, which have changed over the years. A typical set of marks for each Proof House for the years 1925-54 is shown in *Diagram 19a and b* respectively. The marks which superseded them in 1955, and are still in force, are depicted in *Diagram 20a and b*. If a gun has been sent for reproof and

.729″   3¼ TONS

Appears on barrels only

(a)

Appears on action only

(a) *Full Proof Marks, since* 1955, *and currently in force*
London (*for a* 2¾ *in. chambered gun*)

(b)

.729″

3 TONS per ☐″

(b) *Full Proof Marks, since* 1955, *and currently in force*
Birmingham (*for a* 2½ *in. chambered gun*)

**20. Examples of British Proof Marks 1955 and currently in force
of:**
(a) The London Proof House.
(b) The Birmingham Proof House.

passed, the marks shown in *Diagrams 21a and b* will be found, or the current marks will be superimposed on the out-of-date ones. Sometimes a gun may have been sent for special proof, usually to ascertain that it is safe to use with a load heavier than that for which it was originally proved; the respective marks for the two Proof Houses are shown in *Diagrams 22a and b*.

Reciprocal agreements exist with the following countries whereby Britain accepts their standards of proof and they accept hers: Austria, Belgium, Czechoslovakia, France, Italy, Spain, Southern Ireland and West Germany. However the pressures given in kilograms are not directly comparable with ours in tons per sq. in. (t.s.i.). It should be noted that in the U.S.A. there is no official proof of firearms, so American guns offered for sale in the U.K. must bear our proof marks.

(a)

(b)

London Reproving Mark

Birmingham Reproving Mark

21. British Marks denoting re-Proof of:
(a) The London Proof House.
(b) The Birmingham Proof House.

(a)

(b)

London Special Proof

Birmingham Special Proof

22. British Marks denoting Special Proof of:
(a) The London Proof House.
(b) The Birmingham Proof House.

Some old guns may not have the words 'Nitro Proof' stamped on the flats, which means they have been proved for black powder only; it is basically unsafe to use modern nitro cartridges in such a gun, though subject to the advice of a qualified gunsmith it may be worth sending it for and it may pass, nitro proof. If a gun has been fitted with new sleeved barrels, each will be stamped with the word 'sleeved' in addition to the other proof marks.

These are the basic details about proof with which everyone should be conversant. For those who wish to know more, there is an excellent booklet produced jointly by the Proof Houses, entitled *Notes on the Proof of Shotguns and other Small Arms*, which costs only a small sum, and is well worth obtaining and studying.

One final point on keeping a gun in good order; some shooting men are of an enquiring turn of mind, and may be tempted to try and strip down the action and other working parts of a gun. I have already explained how to remove the extractors, and it is equally simple for anyone who can handle a screwdriver efficiently, i.e. without burring the heads of the pins, to remove the locks of a sidelock as may be necessary, e.g. to dry them after shooting in the rain. But unless you are a genuinely competent amateur gunsmith, it is far wiser to leave any further stripping to someone who is properly qualified, or you can easily do more harm than good, like the young enthusiast who takes his watch to pieces, and then finds he cannot put it together again.

Conclusion

When a young soldier joins the Army he is taught similar particulars to all the above about his rifle and ammunition before he is instructed in how to shoot with them, because long experience has shown that this knowledge helps him to be a safer and better shot. If a young soldier is capable of absorbing such information, it should certainly not be too 'technical' or difficult for the average sportsman to grasp, and apply with equal benefit to his own shooting. I feel sure that the failure of many newcomers to game-shooting to acquire this elementary 'know-how' accounts for much of the bad marksmanship and dangerous gun-handling seen in the shooting field to-day.

3 fitting and choice of gun

The Object of Gun Fitting

The purpose of gun fitting is to make the muzzles point where the shooter's eyes are looking when the gun is correctly mounted to his shoulder, so that the shot-pattern is centred on the mark at 40 yds. Many clay-pigeon shots claim that it is unnecessary, and some game-shots, who have managed to shoot tolerably well without ever having had the fit of their gun checked, agree with them. Let us therefore see how the fit of his gun helps the shooter. *Diagram 23* shows in outline the situation if he uses a straight-stocked gun. For simplicity's sake we need consider the line of sight of the right eye only, marked by the line **ET**. If **A** is the point at the shoulder where the stock is bedded home and the muzzles, **B**, are brought into his line of sight, they will point at **C** instead of **T**, because of the displacement of **A** from **E**. This situation could be remedied by the shooter moving his head so as to bring his eye, **E**, into the line **AB**, or in other words by fitting himself to his gun. Down-the-line clay-pigeon shots can to some extent do this successfully because they start 'gun up', as it is known, and then call their target. But these circumstances do not apply in game shooting, where the normal sequence of events is for the target first to appear, and then for the shooter to mount his gun and fire. It is well understood in golf that if, after a player has addressed the ball, he moves his head while making his stroke he will fluff his shot. The same applies in game shooting; if, after he has fixed his eye on his target, the shooter moves his head to fit himself to his gun as be brings it to the shoulder, he too will fluff his shot. But 'skeet' shots may argue that they also start 'gun down', awaiting their target, yet manage to shoot successfully with straight-stocked guns. The reason for this is that skeet-shooting is short-range work, the aim being to break the clay at 20 yds or thereabouts, and heavy charges of shot are used in conjunction with open-bored barrels, three factors which together normally suffice to discount any lack of fit in a gun. In the majority of cases, shortcomings in the fit of a gun only start to become significant at about 30 yds, when targets are hit by the fringe instead of the centre of the pattern, and do not lead to a clean miss until 35 - 40 yds.

So if the game-shooter wishes to be able to deal effectively with quarry at these ranges, and must not move his head to fit himself to the gun, there is only one alternative — to fit the gun to him by adjusting the angle at which the stock is attached to the barrels so that

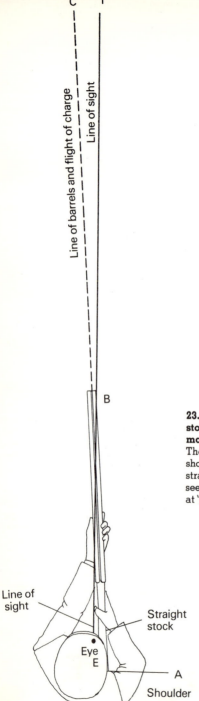

C · T

Line of barrels and flight of charge

Line of sight

B

23. Gun Fitting — why a straight stocked gun, i.e. one with no Cast Off, may not fit the shooter.
The line 'ET' (Eye to Target) is the shooter's line of sight. Because of the straight stock the muzzles, 'B', although seemingly aligned on 'T' actually point at 'C'.

Line of sight

Straight stock

Eye
E

A

Shoulder
A

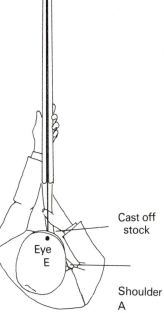

T

Line of sight, and barrels coincides with flight of charge

B

Cast off stock

Eye E

Shoulder A

24. How Cast Off enables the centre-line of the barrels to be made to coincide with the shooter's line of sight, so that the muzzles point where he is looking.

their centre line coincides with his line of sight, as in *Diagram 24*.

Although the amount of adjustment required by most people to achieve this is quite small, it is nevertheless essential if a person is to be able to shoot to the best of his natural ability, and especially if he wants to enjoy the unique satisfaction of dealing successfully with those spectacularly high birds which show up the men from the boys in the field. This applies with equal if not greater force to the less accomplished marksman, as to the most expert, because the former can least afford to place himself under unnecessary handicap.

I hope the above has shown that gun fitting is a genuine aid to the shooter, and disposed conclusively of the fallacy that it is merely an illusory one. Let us now see what it actually entails.

The Critical Measurements

There are three sets of measurements used in gun fitting. They are 'stock length', which is self-explanatory; 'bend', which gives the right elevation, and 'cast off' (or 'cast on' for a left-handed person), which provides the correct lateral line.

The full measurements for stock-length are the distances from the centre of the front trigger to the heel, middle and toe of the butt, as depicted in *Diagram 25*. It is normal practice to refer to the length of a stock in terms of the distance **TB** only, as the shape of the butt is usually standard. However, rather full-chested men and women may require the toe of the butt to be cut back, in which case the distance **TC** is necessary as well, and sometimes that of **TA** also.

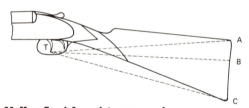

25. How Stock Length is measured.
'TA' is the length from the front trigger to the heel.
'TB' is the length from the front trigger to the middle.
'TC' is the length from the front trigger to the toe.

Two measurements are used to define bend, namely the vertical distances from a horizontal line in rearward extension of the top rib to the comb and bump respectively, as shown in *Diagram 26*. What is commonly referred to as 'standard' bend on proprietary guns is usually $1\frac{1}{2}$ in. at the former, and 2 in. at the latter.

Similarly two measurements are employed to specify cast-off at the same points on the stock, though in this case they are the distances in the lateral plane between the line in rearward extension of the top rib and the comb and bump, as illustrated in *Diagram 27a*. 'Standard' cast-off on proprietary guns is generally $\frac{1}{8}$in. at the comb,

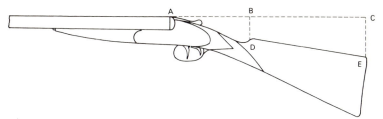

26. How Bend is measured.
The two relevant measurements are to the Comb and Bump, as shown by the lines 'BD' and 'CE' respectively.

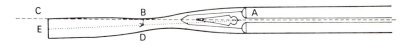

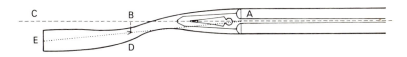

27. How Cast Off is measured.
The two relevant measurements are to the Comb and Bump, as depicted by the lines 'BD' and 'CE' respectively. Diagram 27(b) shows a 'crossover' stock for a left-eyed person shooting off the right shoulder.

and $\frac{1}{4}$ in. at the bump. However it is not uncommon to find shooters who require about double this amount of cast-off, while a right-handed, left-eyed person may require a full 'cross-over' stock, see *Diagram 27b*. Although people claim that they soon become accustomed to the awkwardness of handling a gun so stocked, there are other ways of overcoming left-eye dominance which allow a gun to have a more normal stock, provided of course that the shooter is not blind, or virtually so, in his right eye. These are based on interposing a disc somewhere in the region of the breech to cut off the vision of the left eye when the gun comes to the shoulder. Such a disc may be either a fixture on the left side of the action or stock, or carried on a special extension to a leather handguard (see *Diagram 28*). As the latter requires no modification to the gun itself, which might detract from its secondhand value, an important consideration nowadays, it seems preferable.

Factors affecting Stock Length
Stock-length is the most crucial of the three sets of measurements, because upon its correct assessment those for bend and cast-off are

28. A handguard with disc attachment to cut off left-eye vision.
This can be used to avoid the necessity of a crossover stock, where a
person still has reasonable right-eye vision.

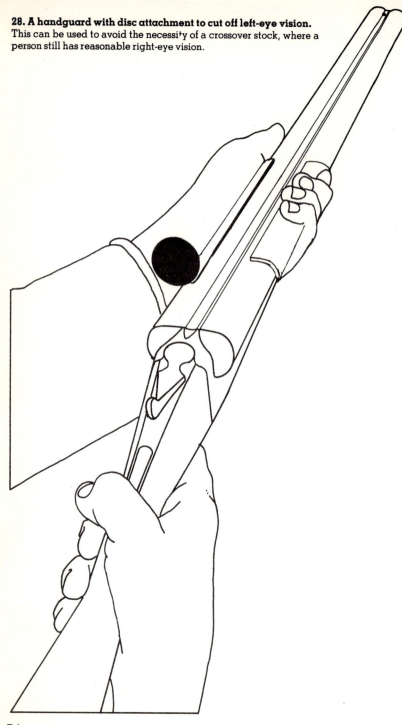

in some degree dependent. As will readily be appreciated the principal factors that determine it are a shooter's length of arm and his bodily physique, but there are others as well.

The style in which a person shoots has significance. Leading players of golf and cricket differ on points of style, and so do leading shooting-men. Thus, some instructors advocate a stance with the left foot more advanced and more nearly in front of the right, than others. The further forward the left foot is placed, the more the left shoulder is swung in front of the right. The consequences of this are shown in *Diagram 29*. The line **ET** represents the shooter's line of sight to the target, that of **AB** his shoulders if he stands plumb square to it with his feet side by side, and that of **CD** the line of his shoulders with his left foot advanced. **A** and **C** are the place at his shoulder to which the stock should be mounted when he shoots. It will be seen that with his shoulders in the line **CD** a longer stock is needed, and because the angle to the line **ET** has been narrowed less cast-off is required, than if his shoulders were in the line **AB**. To illustrate how this applies in practice, down-the-line clay-pigeon shooters have to deal only with a more or less directly going-away target. For this it has been found advantageous to adopt a stance with the left foot markedly in front of the right, and so guns used in this sport have a specially long stock with little or no cast-off.

Some experts recommend a modified down-the-line stance for game shooting, whilst others advocate a squarer one. The former invariably advise a longer stock than the latter. The question of which is the better is dealt with in chapter 5. The point which should be understood is that if a person is first taught to shoot in one style and then another, it may well entail a change in the fit of his gun. To avoid this contingency arising, it is therefore just as important as in golf or cricket to take the trouble to find a shooting-school or coach in whom you believe you can have confidence, and stick to the technique you are taught.

Many people go to a shooting-school to be fitted for a gun in spring or summer, and if the weather is fine arrive in shirt sleeves or a lightweight suit, whereas on a winter's day at the covertside they will be wearing a heavy jacket over a thick sweater. This can make a full $\frac{1}{4}$-in. difference in the length of stock required, so clothes that will enable one to dress as for shooting should be taken on such an occasion.

A further consideration affecting stock-length is gun weight. A heavy gun will need a rather shorter stock than a lighter one. Thus if a man has a $7\frac{3}{4}$-lb. magnum for wildfowling it may need to be stocked a $\frac{1}{4}$ in. or so shorter than his $6\frac{1}{2}$-lb. game gun to achieve as satisfactory a fit. Conversely, if he has a 28-bore to take on evening strolls in pursuit of a rabbit for the pot, he may require at least an extra $\frac{1}{4}$ in. on the stock.

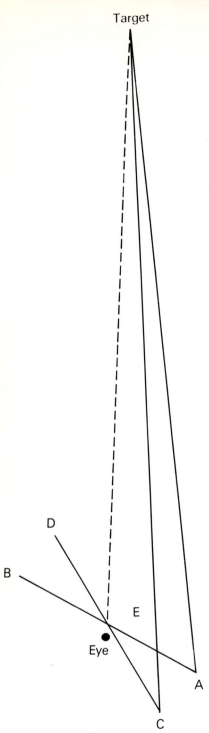

Target

29. How stance affects the fit of a gun.
The line 'AB' represents that of the shooter's shoulders if he stands square to his target. If the left foot is advanced his shoulders will move into the line 'CD', thus affecting both stock length and cast-off required.

56

Factors affecting Bend

The length of a person's neck and the shape of his shoulders are the main, though not sole, factors that determine how much bend he will need on his stock.

When a gun-barrel is fired, a phenomenon known as 'barrel flip' occurs; if the flip is positive the charge will be thrown high, and if negative, low. Which happens depends on the length of the barrel. It has been discovered that with 25-in. barrels the flip is positive, and with 30-in. ones, negative, the former centring the charge about 10 in. above a given mark at 40 yds and the latter about 10 in. below. Bend is increased to make a gun shoot lower, and decreased to make it shoot higher. So if a person changes to shorter barrels he may find more bend is necessary on his stock to counteract the difference in barrel flip. The more rigid the construction of the barrels, the less the flip. Thus in an over-and-under, when the bottom barrel is fired there is virtually no flip, and such a gun with 30-in. barrels will require more bend than an equivalent side-by-side.

A gun should shoot to the mark, and it should be understood what this means. Some people talk airily about the supposed advantage of having a gun with 'high shooting qualities'. But such a gun would prove a positive handicap in dealing with incoming ground game or high going-away birds. However, it has been found from experience that the greatest benefit is derived from having a gun which centres its pattern 4 in. above the mark at 40 yds, and this is what a properly fitting game-gun should do. The equivalent figure for 'trap' guns for down-the-line clay-pigeon shooting is 9 in., which explains why such guns have less bend than game guns.

Although a shooter's eyes should be fixed on the target to the exclusion of all else when he is taking a shot, they will subconsciously register the centre-line of the barrels, i.e. the top rib, as it moves into his line of vision. Thus a top rib that is swept down low between the muzzles will have the same effect as a low foresight on a rifle, and result in the shot going higher than would a rib that stands rather 'proud' at the muzzles like the Churchill quick-sighting tapered rib, or a raised flat, filecut rib. So the type of rib on a gun can also affect the amount of bend required by the shooter.

Factors affecting Cast Off

The chief factors in deciding how much cast off is needed are the shooter's line of sight, and his width of shoulder. How stance can affect the issue had already been described. It has always seemed to me that the part played by the eyes in shotgun shooting has been little understood even by some leading instructors, and hence all kinds of myths have been perpetuated in teaching people how to shoot. So important do I believe it that these should be dispelled and the functioning of the eyes properly appreciated, that I have dealt with the subject separately in chapter 8, including the matter relevant here of a person's line of sight.

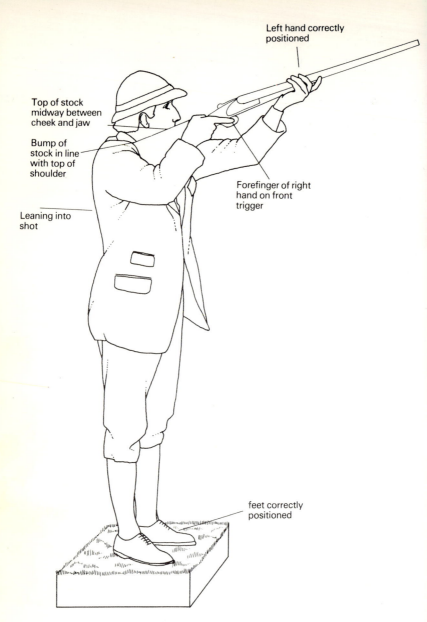

Left hand correctly positioned

Top of stock midway between cheek and jaw

Bump of stock in line with top of shoulder

Leaning into shot

Forefinger of right hand on front trigger

feet correctly positioned

30. Side view of a shooter with a properly fitting gun.

Miscellaneous Matters

We are now in a position to see how a properly fitting gun should look in the hands of a shooter. The side view depicted in *Diagram 30* illustrates the following points:

a. The butt is bedded against the upper part of the pectoral muscle of the chest, as it should be.

b. The heel of the butt, or bump, is in line with the top of the shoulder.

c. The top line of the stock has come to rest against the shooter's cheek, mid-way between jawbone and cheekbone.

d. The hands are able to take their correct holds (see ch.4) easily and comfortably.

e. The shooter is able to lean his body slightly forward into his shot, thus helping to absorb recoil without discomfort.

f. The feet are correctly placed (see ch.4).

A frontal, or bird's eye view is shown in *Diagram 31*, from which it will be seen that, as the shooter is right-eyed, his eye is fractionally above the centre of the breech, and the muzzles are pointing straight at the target.

31. Front view of a shooter with a properly fitting gun.
The shooter's eye appears to be fractionally above the breech, and the 'Target' is looking straight down the muzzles.

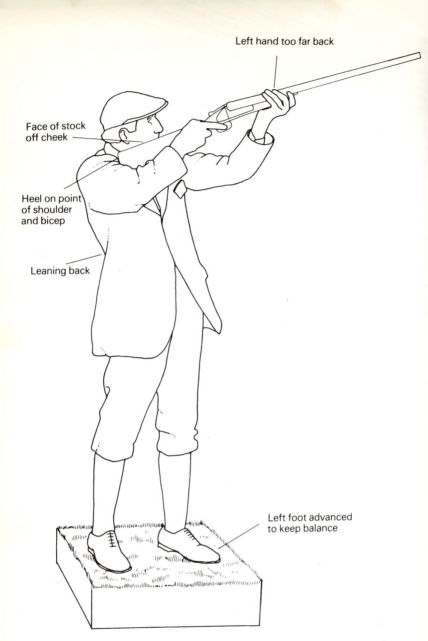

Left hand too far back

Face of stock
off cheek

Heel on point
of shoulder
and bicep

Leaning back

Left foot advanced
to keep balance

32. Faults induced by too long a stock — side view.

Let us now compare this with what happens when the stock is too long, as illustrated in *Diagram 32* which reveals the following:

a. The butt is bedded on the point of the shoulder and the upper part of the bicep, which in the course of firing only a few rounds can cause painful bruising.

b. Because the shooter has had to pull his shoulder back to accommodate the butt, it has snagged his jacket, and is too low.

c. Consequent on b. above, his cheek is off the stock.

d. He has had to reach out with both hands, but even so his left is still too far back.

e. Pulling his right shoulder back has forced him to lean backwards, which will aggravate the effects of recoil.

f. Because he has leaned back, he has had to move his right foot rearwards to keep his balance.

From the front, (*Diagram 33*) it will be seen that his eye is well above and to the side of, the breech, while the muzzles point high and to the right of his target.

Although for purposes of illustrating clearly the problems posed by too long a stock a rather exaggerated example has been taken, it should be realised that a stock need only be ¼ in. too long for all this to be liable to happen in some degree.

Too short a stock is a rather lesser evil, and can be countered by holding the left hand further forward. However, even if this is done, the gun will not come so readily to the correct place at the shoulder, and erratic shooting is likely to result.

These are the fundamental factors in gun fitting. I hope I have shown that finding the right combination of stock-length, bend, and cast-off is not always as simple a matter as it might superficially appear to be, and especially for someone unaware of the complications involved. In my view it is a job for an expert, and is best entrusted to a qualified instructor at a reputable shooting-school. Quite apart from the matters discussed in this chapter there are others less specific, but no less of account, if a person is to be able to enjoy his sport with a gun to the full. Again it requires an expert to give sound advice on these. They are discussed below.

MATCHING THE GUN TO THE SHOOTER & HIS SPORT

General Considerations

Striking the right note in respect of weight, barrel-length, and balance is essential in acquiring any gun, irrespective of whether it is principally for shooting driven-game or wildfowl. Those who have to rely on one gun for all their sport will seek in vain for a weapon that is ideal for every occasion (what has already been said in chapter 2 about loads, shot sizes, and choke should have made this clear). However, if careful consideration is given to the above points it is remarkable what a satisfactory compromise can be achieved with a well chosen, ordinary 2½-in. chambered 12-bore game-gun. If the owner of such a gun is prepared to exercise a bit more cunning and work a little harder to get on terms with his quarry in certain circumstances, as for example in the pursuit of wildfowl, he should be able to enjoy such a wide variety of good sport that he will only rarely feel at a genuine disadvantage for lack of a more supposedly ideal weapon.

Gun Weight

Nobody, especially a rough shooter, wants to be encumbered with an unnecessarily heavy gun. As explained earlier, the heaviest shot-load it is required to handle dictates the minimum weight of a gun. A person of average height and physique ought to be able to use a 12-bore of 6lb 8 - 10oz. without discomfort for a full day's shooting. A weapon of this weight will allow him to use the heavier load of the 'Maximum' cartridge for long-range shooting with large shot, such as wildfowling may demand, without suffering excessive recoil. But for some time the trend has been to build 12-bore game-guns rather lighter, that is around 6lb 4 - 6oz. But such guns are designed for use with the standard load, and if this is exceeded recoil in my experience becomes unpleasant after firing only comparatively few consecutive shots. So if a person opts for a light, modern 12-bore, he must accept that this limits him to the use of light loads. Although guns of this kind are an undoubted advantage to many people who are mainly concerned with the shooting of driven-game, there are some tall men of robust physique who find a heavier gun gives them better control of the timing of their shots, i.e. in synchronising the moment at which the muzzles come to bear on the target with that at which they intend to pull the trigger. In fact just as a man can have too heavy a gun to shoot his best, so he can also have too light a one. As the virtues of light guns, for those whose shooting needs they will meet, have been widely extolled in recent years, and we are all inclined to be slaves to fashion, this point is worth remembering when setting out to acquire a gun. Certainly if the advice of a qualified shooting-coach on this score is at odds with any preconceived ideas a person may have of his own, he may be better advised to revise his ideas than ignore that advice.

There are some people besides young shots who, on account of their small stature and/or slight physique, will be better served with a gun lighter than a standard 12-bore. They have a number of options. A 12-bore to handle the 1-oz. lead can be built to a minimum weight of 5lb. 14oz. But anyone who is prone to suffer from the ill-effects of recoil should have a gun a little heavier than the minimum for a given load — say, in this case, one of 6 lb. A more significant saving in weight can be obtained by turning to a 16-bore, or 2-in. chambered 12-bore. The latter are delightful to shoot with, having a notably soft recoil, which makes them excellent guns for ladies or elderly sportsmen. However they handle a slightly lighter load than a 16-bore which places them at a marginal disadvantage to it. The weights to which 16-bores and 2-in. chambered 12-bores are

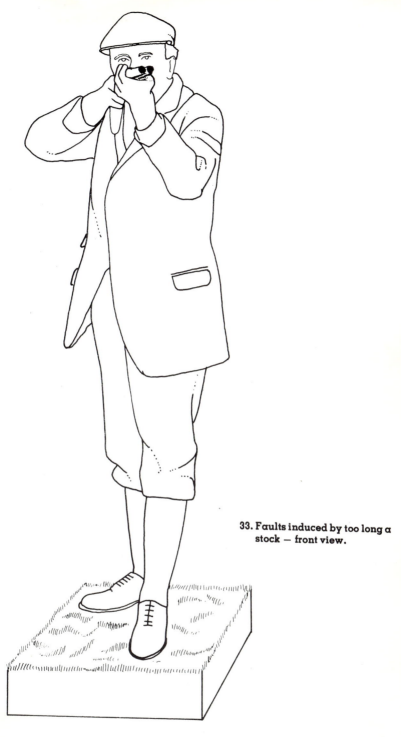

33. Faults induced by too long a
stock — front view.

usually built are $5\frac{1}{2}$ - 6 lb. and $5\frac{1}{4}$ - $5\frac{3}{4}$ lb. respectively. There is of course some loss of performance compared to a standard 12-bore, but if the relevant standard load of No.7 shot is used instead of No.6 for small game, an improved cylinder-barrel of both a 16-bore and a 2-in. chambered 12-bore will give adequate pattern-densities at 40 yds, as also with No.4 shot for larger quarry such as geese and hares. However patterns of No.8 shot for snipe will lose their effective density at around 35 yds. The loss in performance is therefore slight.

Quite a number of sportsmen shoot driven-game in masterly style with a 20-bore, so much so that 12-bore users may appear put to shame. A $2\frac{1}{2}$-in. chambered 20-bore usually weighs about $5\frac{1}{2}$ lb. and fires a standard load of $1\frac{3}{16}$ oz., which is only $\frac{1}{16}$ oz. less than that of the 2-in. chambered 12-bore, but $\frac{1}{4}$ oz. less than that of the standard 12-bore. Using No.7 shot a 20-bore improved-cylinder barrel should just shoot a sufficiently dense pattern at 40 yds to ensure that a bird the size of a partridge is cleanly killed. But in practice it is rightly accepted that the effective range limit of a 20-bore is only 35 yds. Its smaller charge also curtails its effectiveness in dealing with bigger or smaller quarry, requiring heavier shot or denser patterns respectively.

On balance therefore the best light-gun alternative seems to me to be the 2 in.-chambered 12-bore, as it offers the greatest weight advantage for the least significant loss of performance.

Barrel Length

Since it was demonstrated that the rather lower ballistics given by shorter barrels do not significantly impair effective performance in the shooting-field, the trend has been to shorter-barelled guns. This was lent impetus by the late Robert Churchill's advocacy of 25-in. barrels.

The case for short barrels rests primarily on two grounds:

a. They facilitate the making of lighter guns.

b. They impart better, more lively handling qualities, which assist the shooter to get quickly on to his target.

As regards the former, it has already been explained that the weight of a gun is governed by the size of the charge it is intended to handle. So although this claim is true, it is only so subject to this qualification.

As far as the latter is concerned, shorter barrels certainly do impart livelier handling qualities, but what is all right for one person may prove too lively for another. Shooting-coaches are widely agreed that as a rule tall men will shoot their best with long barrels to harmonise with the long stock they need, and that similarly, small men will do so with short barrels. Thus for a man over 6ft tall, 30-in. barrels are considered advisable, and for one barely over 5 ft, 25- or 26-in. ones. As the majority of men are nearer 6 ft than 5 ft, this explains the predominance of 28-in. barrels. It has been found that for a man to handle barrels shorter than the length appropriate to his height successfully demands greater skill and sharper reflexes than many can hope to acquire or possess, and in consequence they merely lead to erratic performance. From my own experience of shooting with guns with different lengths of barrel, I believe this is basically correct. If however a person is an above-average marksman who shoots frequently, and so is always in practice, then I believe he may indeed benefit from using shorter barrels, e.g. 26-in. barrels instead of 28-in., because his ability should enable him to turn the greater liveliness to good account. Similarly anyone accustomed to 30-in. barrels might well change to 28-in. ones, but I would be very hesitant in recommending 26 in. to such a man, because in my opinion the change would be too dramatic, and one step down (i.e. of 2 in.) is enough.

Now a word about 25-in. barrels; thanks to Robert Churchill these have achieved considerable prominence. Many shooting-coaches and members of the gun trade are of the opinion that such barrels are just too short, and that it is unwise to go below 26 in. This is a highly controversial question. I have known people who have shot well, and consistently so, with 25-in. barrelled guns, but also others for whom they have proved disastrous. It is therefore a barrel-length about which I have unresolved doubts, except for short people. I certainly do not believe it is an infallible aid to better shooting for anyone, as is sometimes claimed.

Balance

I consider balance second only in importance to good shooting-characteristics in a gun, i.e. its ability to shoot consistently first-class quality lethal patterns with the loads for which it has been regulated. The term 'balance' embraces the dynamic handling-qualities of a gun as well as its static point of balance. The latter should be in the region of the crosspin, and is of small consequence compared to the former.

To impart good balance — i.e. lively handling qualities — gun-makers always try to concentrate the weight between the hands, as they describe it, that is between approximately the loop on the barrels and the safety-catch at the rear of the action. But I believe this is only part of the story, and that it is correct distribution of weight throughout the length of a gun, rather than mere concentration of the greater part of it centrally, that is the key to good balance. The force of this contention will be appreciated if you compare the lively 'feel' of a well-balanced gun with another of the same weight or nearly so, which isn't, and handles like a weaver's beam.

It will be readily understood how a combination of long barrels and a short stock can make the achievement of good balance more difficult. People sometimes inherit a best gun, or pair of guns with 30-in. barrels: if it is necessary to have the stock shortened materially, to fit the new owner, it may also be advisable to consider shortening the barrels to harmonise with the shorter stock, especially if the person concerned has been accustomed to shooting with shorter barrels. If the gunmaker consulted advises that cutting down the barrels is impracticable, or having new sleeved barrels of the right length is not a sound proposition, it may be best to exchange the gun for another that is more suitable. I have known cases where, although the original maker has altered the guns in question to the best of his ability to fit the beneficiary, the latter has never shot as well with them as with a weapon of humbler origin he used before. So although inherited guns may have a strong sentimental value, practical considerations should be given precedence if you are to have a gun with which you can shoot your best.

The moment of inertia of the section of the barrels in front of a shooter's left hand is important in providing the stability he needs in order to judge his timing correctly. If this section is too light or too short or both, he will find that the muzzles tend to whip about all over the place, and as a result his shooting is erratic. In my experience the overall weight of a gun is the crucial factor, in that the greater this is, the bigger the effort that has to be made to lift it and provide the impulsion to the barrels, and so the greater the inertia of the forward section of the barrels needs to be to give the requisite stability. It follows therefore that with heavy guns relatively long barrels help to promote good balance. As an example of how this may apply in practice, I shoot with a 12-bore game-gun which weighs 6½ lb. and has 26-in. barrels. Formerly I have tried both 30- and 28-in. barrels, but there is no doubt that 26-in. suit me best, and I feel completely at home with them using a gun of this weight. However for wildfowling I use a semi-magnum weighing just under 7 lb. which has 28-in. barrels, and the longer barrels seem appropriate to this heavier gun. Some years ago I was shown a 12-bore magnum which was around 8lb. and had 25-in. barrels. Although the fit of the stock was approximately right for me, it felt a very cumbersome, ill-balanced weapon, because there seemed too little length and weight of barrel in front of the left hand to counterbalance its overall weight. In consequence when I attempted some 'dry' practice with snap caps, my timing was all awry.

Balance is very much a personal matter, and what feels exactly right for one individual may not be so for another, even though they may be of similar physique. I have tried to avoid using technical jargon, because in my view it tends to confuse the ordinary sportsman; for example to talk of the 'radius of gyration' of a gun when it is mounted to the shoulder conveys an impression that it should somehow be rotated or cartwheeled, which is precisely what should be avoided. Also just because an engineer's sums show that the balance of two guns, which differ in certain characteristics, is the same, it does not follow that a person trying to shoot with them will find that they 'feel' the same, so complex is the relationship between balance, barrel-length, and weight.

In conclusion, if you possess what seems to you a really well balanced gun of acceptable weight, with which you believe you can shoot as well as you are ever likely to, treat it as a pearl beyond price. Be very hesitant about exchanging it for a more fashionable, lighter or shorter-barrelled weapon, because it could easily prove a change for the worse, not the better. Equally, if you wish to acquire a gun, take the best advice you can as to the specifications you should seek, and don't allow any glib salesman to persuade you that any maker's name, however famous, will compensate for material shortcomings in these. As is said of women and horses, there are as many good fish in the sea as ever came out of it, and if you persist in your search for the gun you really want, you may be sure your efforts will ultimately be rewarded. If you have been well advised in the beginning, it will be well worth any delay and extra trouble involved. Always remember, whatever the name on a gun and the merits it may possess, it will only kill as well and often as your standard of marksmanship allows. So we will now move on to this problem.

STANCE AND FOOTWORK

General

Good game-shooting is just as much a matter of adept coordination of the actions of the hands with the dictates of the eyes, and of using the feet correctly to assist in the taking of shots, as is the playing of good golf or good tennis. In all three, shots can be successfully accomplished without the aid of footwork, but this severely limits what the shooter/player could otherwise achieve. So although on occasions, such as when walking up snipe or lying in wait for wildfowl, a shooter may have to manage as best he can without being able to use his feet to help, it will benefit him to employ them to full advantage whenever circumstances allow.

Stance

A tennis player awaiting service from his opponent will stand with his feet approximately level with each other and not too far apart, with his weight equally balanced on the balls of both feet, so that he can move right, left or forwards with equal facility to take his shot. A shooter also should adopt a well balanced stance whilst awaiting his shot so that he can deal as easily with a target to right or left as one in front. But when he 'plays' his shot, he has to withstand the recoil of his gun. When a person is first given a gun to shoot with, he almost invariably puts his left foot well forward to assist his capacity to do this. However, the further forward the left foot is placed, the more restricted becomes the arc over which he can swing to right or left. So to retain maximum flexibility, a shooter should keep his left foot as nearly back on a level with his right as he can and still shoot in comfort. To meet these conditions the feet should therefore be placed as in *Diagram 34*, that is with the left foot echeloned a little ahead of the right, the toes pointing slightly outwards, and the heels about 4 in. apart. A man of over 6 ft. may need a rather wider

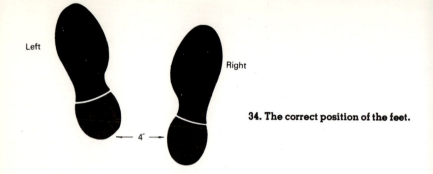

Left

Right

34. The correct position of the feet.

4″

stance, and a small one a somewhat narrower one. While awaiting a shot, keep the weight equally balanced on both feet.

In another stance that is taught at some shooting-schools, the left foot is placed farther forward, and more in line ahead of the right with the weight mainly on the front foot. In my view the basic flaw in this is that the shooter starts off balance, and if he swings briskly round for a shot to his right — involving the transfer of weight on to his right leg — so narrow is this stance that he is liable to over-balance. However there is no gainsaying that some game-shots who use it, shoot very well, though it has always seemed to me better suited to someone who is primarily a competition clay-pigeon shot, and from my experience of both stances that described previously is the better one for game shooting.

Footwork

Having discovered how to position our feet, let us now see how to use them. For a target to his front at head height, or thereabouts, the shooter should merely lean slightly forward as he mounts the gun to his shoulder, thus placing more weight on his front foot, no movement being required. For a shot really low in front at, say, a target downhill such as walked-up grouse sometimes offer, you will need to lean farther forward into your shot, and as the weight transfers to the left foot the right heel should rise as shown in *Diagram 35*. If the ground permits, the left foot may also be slid 2 or 3 in. forward as your weight goes on to it.

The higher a target approaches from the front, the closer it must be allowed to come in, so that it is properly within range. With really high birds the feet should be used as depicted in *Diagram 36*. As the shooter follows the target with his eyes and raises his gun, the consequent rearward incline of his body brings his weight smoothly and progressively back on to the right foot, the left heel rising as the backswing increases. There is no need to move the right foot back for this shot, nor if your stance is correct to begin with should there be any tendency to do so.

As regards dealing with shots to right and left — a right-handed

35. Use of the feet for a shot low in front.
As the weight goes forward on to the left leg the right heel lifts off the ground.

shooter normally disposes of those to his left with greater natural fluency than ones to his right, just as a tennis or squash player is usually stronger on his forehand than his backhand. As a person starts to mount his gun for a shot to his left he should begin to pivot

36. Use of the feet for a shot overhead.
As the weight comes back on to the right
leg, the left heel lifts off the ground.

37. Use of the feet for a shot to the left.
The weight goes on to the left leg, and as the shooter pivots at the hips the right heel rises.

his body about the hips, simultaneously transferring his weight to his left leg. As his angle of turn increases, causing his right heel to lift, he should pivot on his right toe and left heel (see *Diagram 37*). However, in practice, unless the ground on which he is standing is hard and dead level, it will in my experience be impracticable to slide the left foot round on the axis of the heel without it catching the odd small stone or twig, which can easily cause a momentary loss of balance as his weight is virtually all on that foot. The left ankle will therefore often perforce have to be the pivotal point of the left leg, and the slightly inhibiting effect this has on the attainable arc of turn accepted.

For a shot to the right, the same sequence of events should be observed (see *Diagram 38a*), only this time the weight goes on to the

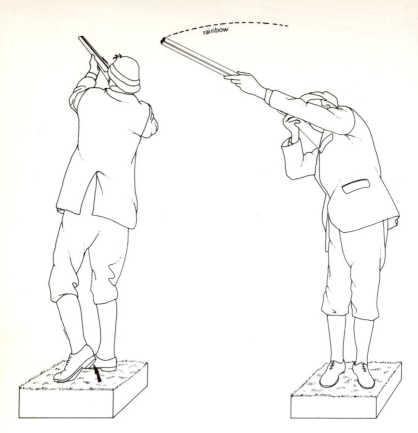

38. Use of the feet for a shot to the right.
The weight goes on to the right leg, and as the shooter pivots at the hips the left heel rises. If the shooter stands 'flat footed', as depicted in 38(b), the angle through which he can turn is restricted, and to increase it he has to bend over, causing the muzzles to 'rainbow'.

right leg, and it is the left heel that rises as the angle of turn increases. But many people find it much more awkward shooting to their right, and probably because this impairs their self-confidence achieve comparatively little success with targets to this flank. A common cause of their failure is that they stand 'flat footed', that is they do not allow their left heel to lift so that their left toe can pivot as they turn. In consequence the angle through which they can turn at the hips becomes restricted, and in order to get farther round they have to bend at the waist, causing their right shoulder to drop and their gun barrels to cant and travel in an arc instead of straight along the line of flight of their target. This is known as 'rainbowing' with the gun (*Diagram 38b*), and causes the shot to go low and behind. It can of course happen just as well with a shot to the left if the right heel isn't raised, but in practice this seems to occur much less frequently.

72

A games player automatically braces his legs, body and arms as he makes his shot in order to get his full power behind it. A shooter should similarly brace himself as he takes a shot in order to absorb the recoil of the gun. When a person shoots spontaneously this is done instinctively, and if he is using a gun with a properly matched load, the recoil is unnoticed. If he takes an 'aimed' shot at a stationary target and forgets to brace himself as he pulls the trigger, he will be made only too well aware of the force of the recoil, and how it can throw him off balance for a quick second barrel. This momentary bracing of the legs, etc. as the shot is taken is therefore just as much a part of good footwork in shooting as in games, and if this is understood by the novice right from the start will quickly become a natural reflex action.

These are the elements of good footwork based on a sound, well-balanced stance. It will of course always pay a shooter to make things easy for himself by turning to face his target if time allows. But when it doesn't, if he is a normally supple person the footwork described above, properly performed, should enable him to cover effectively an arc extending well round to his right or left rear.

USE OF THE HANDS

General
Taking a correct grip with his hands on the gun, and then using them properly in making his shot are matters of no less importance to a shooter than a golfer with his club.

Position of the Hands
When a person comes to the 'ready' position prior to taking a shot, as described in the next chapter, his right hand should hold the small of the stock, as shown in *Diagram 39*, and his left grasp the barrels in the region of the top of the fore-end, as depicted in *Diagram 40*, (see also *Diagram 30*).

The right hand should be well round the 'hand' of the stock with the forefinger extended along the trigger-guard so that the pad of the top joint can comfortably reach the front trigger when the moment comes to fire. The side of the top joint of the thumb should rest against the rear of the safety-catch, so that as the gun is being brought to the shoulder it can be readily pushed forward. It is wrong to use the flat of the thumb because it slightly impairs the grip with this hand, and also in easing forward the slide the top of the thumb may override the stud and come to rest against the end of the top lever, which on recoil can cause a bruised or split thumb.

The left hand should grip the barrels firmly in the region of the top of the fore-end, with the thumb pointing straight down the side of the left barrel to assist in aiming the muzzles correctly. The tips of the fingers should not encroach over the top of the right barrel; if

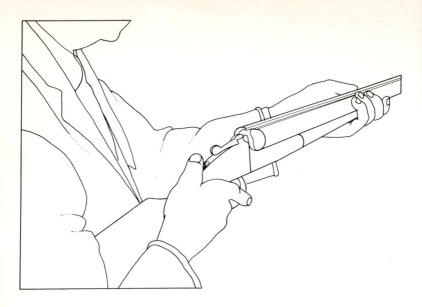

39. Correct right-hand hold in the 'Ready' position.

they do, the centre-line of the barrels, as noted subconsciously by the shooter's eyes just before he fires, will no longer be that of the top rib, but a line nearer the centre of the left barrel (see *Diagram 41*), thus causing an error of aim.

The exact place at which the left hand holds the barrels should be found by trial and error. It should be where the gun feels as well balanced as possible in both hands and when it is mounted to the shoulder the left arm is not over-extended or too cramped.

Use of the Hands
In game-shooting each hand performs two roles. In conjunction with the arms both act as levers to lift the gun to the shoulder, and otherwise move it as the shooter requires. In addition the right operates the triggers, while the left guides the muzzles on to the target. Thus the left hand plays the key role, and it is the right that must follow its lead and work in harmony with it. I do not therefore like the hold advocated by some coaches in which the left forefinger is pointed down the line of the bottom rib, because it weakens the grip of that hand and the thumb is inclined to stray over the top of the left barrel creating a similar situation to that described above if the finger-tips encroach over the right barrel. The left thumb, when aligned along the side of the left barrel (see Diagram 40), serves just as adequately as a pointer.

At the moment of firing, as the right hand is pulling the stock into the shoulder, the left should be pushing out, so that the left arm takes a share of the recoil. By helping to distribute the effect of recoil in this way it is not only made less noticeable, but disturbance of aim is reduced, allowing quicker, more accurate second-barrel shooting.

When the shooter starts to move the gun from the 'ready' position to his shoulder he will instinctively tighten his grip with both hands, and again as he actually fires. This also assists the arms to absorb some of the recoil, and prevent it all from impinging on the right shoulder, again materially helping to reduce noticeability. When shooting for the first time, probably at a stationary target, a novice is often encouraged to do so with the gun deliberately placed at his shoulder, after which he aims and fires. As a result of 'shooting by numbers' in this way he frequently slackens the grip of his hands once the gun is at his shoulder and fails to tighten it again as he is about to pull the trigger, so that the full impact of the recoil falls on his shoulder and cheek, and is most unpleasantly noticeable. As this may well induce a tendency to flinch (i.e. lift the head off the stock at the instant of firing) — a fault that is most difficult subsequently

40. Correct left-hand hold in the 'Ready' position.

to eradicate — it is important that a person, especially a youngster, should be conversant with how to use his hands properly before he is taken out to shoot for the first time. This, and other basic elements of gun-handling can be readily learnt by 'dry' practice with the aid of snap caps, as will be more fully explained in the following chapter.

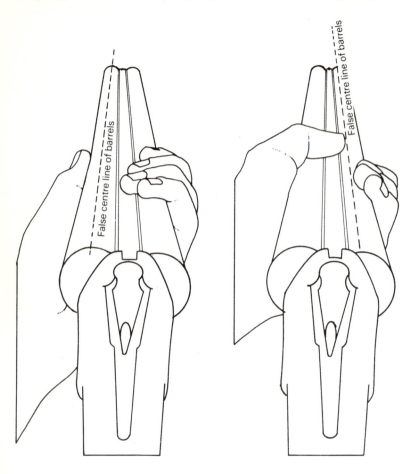

41. Why the fingers or thumb of the left hand must not be allowed to encroach over the top of the barrels.
The false centre-line of the barrels subconsciously picked up by the eyes causes an error of aim, which may induce a miss at a high bird.

GUN MOUNTING AND HANDLING

General
The gun must be mounted correctly to the shoulder for every shot, see *Diagram 30*. Unless it is, the centre-line of the barrels and the

shooter's line of sight will not coincide, as they should with a properly fitting gun, and errors of aim will result. Proficient gun mounting is therefore necessary to gain full advantage from such a gun.

Clearly the shorter the distance over which the stock has to travel to the shoulder the better the chance of the butt arriving at the right place, and the easier it is to coordinate this with the pointing of the muzzles in the right direction. Every sportsman who has been caught napping, with his gun over his arm when a target has appeared unexpectedly, will appreciate the force of this and the advantage of being able to bring his gun to a 'ready' position prior to taking a shot. That devised by the late Robert Churchill has always seemed to me best to meet the shooter's needs.

The Ready Position

Diagram 42 illustrates this 'ready' position. The shooter's eyes are fixed on his target, or where he anticipates it will appear; his hands are positioned as described in the previous section. The gun has been raised so that the butt of the stock is cuddled between his upper arm and the side of his chest, thus relieving the hands of some of the burden; the muzzles point where his eyes are looking. His feet

42. The 'Ready' Position.
Note that the muzzles are pointed where the shooter is looking.

are placed as in *Diagram 34*, and his weight is comfortably balanced on both.

As his eyes follow the target, his hands should instinctively adjust the tilt of the barrels, so that the muzzles conform. This phase is equivalent to that of 'addressing the ball' at golf, and like a golfer, a shooter must from this point onwards not move his head independently of his body until he has completed his shot, or in other words he must remain 'stiff necked'.

When his target has come within range and he decides the moment has arrived to take his shot, he should start to push the gun forward with his left hand assisted by the right. When the heel of the butt is clear of his armpit, the gun should be raised with both hands, and then the butt pulled home to the correct place at the shoulder with the right hand, the shoulder thrusting fractionally forward to meet the butt. Although I have described this by stages, it should in fact be all one smoothly flowing, briskly executed movement, just like a golfer's swing. His eyes should remain fixed on the target throughout, and his hands keep the muzzles bearing on it. The precise timing of the movement will be dictated by the eyes, as explained in the next chapter. The safety-catch should be pushed forward as the gun is moved forward. The trigger should be pulled immediately after the stock has bedded home against the shoulder.

If for any reason the shot is not completed the gun should be

43. Two unsatisfactory ready positions.

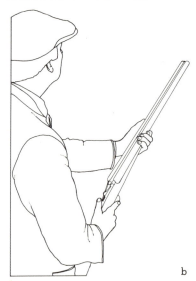

a

b

From both these positions the gun has to be cartwheeled when the butt is mounted to the shoulder, making precision in this important respect more difficult.

brought back to the ready position and the safety-catch reapplied, while another target is selected. If there is a pause during which the shooter has no target in view, but feels he should remain in a state of semi-readiness rather than adopt a rest position, he should lower the muzzles so that they point to the ground, and slightly relax the grip of his hands.

The salient virtue of this ready position is that it provides for such a short, simple movement to transfer the gun to the shoulder. This can be readily mastered with only a minimum of practice, and then it should be exceptional for any fault to occur in usage in the field.

Other ready positions are taught and used; two fairly commonly seen are shown in *Diagrams 43a and 43b*. With both of these the gun has to be cartwheeled in order to bring the butt to the shoulder, which makes it more difficult to synchronise with the muzzles coming to bear on the target. In the case of the position shown in Diagram 43a, the butt is liable to mount too high, which results in the muzzles pointing too low, while with the position depicted in Diagram 43b the situation is reversed, as illustrated in *Diagrams 44a and 44b*. Also in both of these ready positions the hands alone bear the whole weight of the gun, and being rather farther from the body (*Diagram 42*), cannot exercise such precise control over its subsequent movements, thus increasing the possibility of error in actual mounting. I do not therefore consider either of these or any variation of them will serve the shooter as well as the ready position advocated above.

Application of our ready position in practice is not restricted merely to driven-game shooting, or other occasions on which the individual is a standing gun. It can equally well be used on appropriate occasions when walking up game — for example on snipe ground or in rough cover where rabbits are lying out, when one's quarry may flush at any moment and slick gun-mounting can make all the difference between a shot well taken, or one not taken at all. I would emphasise that in these circumstances the muzzles should still point where the shooter is looking, that is at the ground about 20 yds to his front, or as the case may be. It can also be employed when shooting over dogs, irrespective of whether the occasion involves a brace of setters on a grouse moor, or one man and his German shorthaired pointer on enclosed land. Wildfowlers with their heavier artillery certainly do not lack opportunities where it can be used to advantage. In fact covert-shooter, rough-shooter, and wildfowler will all benefit from incorporating this ready position in their normal shooting drill. It need only involve the briefest of pauses, that with practice will cause a negligible loss of time in taking a shot, which will be more than compensated for by better results gained from the greater precision of one's gun mounting.

So I would unhesitatingly recommend all those wishing to become accomplished marksmen to make time to practice it with snap caps in the home as well as live ammunition in the field; it will be well spent.

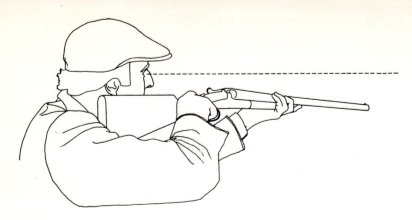

44. The likely consequences of adopting the ready positions in the previous Diagram.

(a) If the butt has to be cartwheeled through a materially greater arc than the muzzles it is liable to mount too high.

(b) Conversely, if the muzzles have to be cartwheeled through a materially greater arc than the butt, the latter is liable to mount too low.

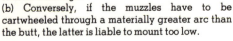

Miscellaneous Gun Handling

Mastery of the ready position and movement of the gun from there to the shoulder are indispensable preliminaries to learning how to shoot. It is desirable that the aspiring game shot should also know at this stage what to do when he first picks up a gun, and how to carry it. The other elements of gun-handling with which he should become equally familiar can be taught as he progresses with his shooting. As they are all intimately concerned with safety in the shooting-field, they are dealt with separately in a later chapter devoted to this subject.

Action on Picking Up a Gun

Your first action on picking up a shotgun or any other firearm should invariably be to prove whether ot not it is loaded by opening and inspecting the breech, and if applicable checking the magazine as well. In the Army this used to be the first piece of arms drill a recruit was taught after he had been issued with a rifle, and grizzled old musketry instructors threatened and exacted dire penalties for failure to observe this precaution, so that in a very short while it became a natural reflex action on picking up or being handed a weapon. In the handling of sporting arms it is no less important, though reliance has to be placed on a sportsman's good sense rather than an N.C.O.'s eagle eye to train himself so that it is performed as a matter of habit. It is certainly the first lesson anyone starting a novice or young shot on his shooting career should inculcate in his pupil.

Never assume a gun is unloaded, and never accept anyone else's assurance to this effect. I have twice picked up a gun in a house, having been told in each case that it was unloaded, only to find on checking that there were cartridges in the breech: it is a most unpleasant experience. With a conventional double-barrelled shotgun opening and inspecting the breech is very simply and quickly effected; with magazine weapons it is slightly more complex and takes a little longer, but there is never any excuse for not doing it. Yet failure to make this basic check is a continuing cause of accidents with firearms, a number of which are fatal.

If you hand a gun to another person, you should either do so with the breech open, or if this is impracticable, first show him the empty breech, then close it, and pass the weapon to him.

You should know the above, and put it into effect from the very first time you take out a gun to go shooting, irrespective of whether this is at a shooting-school, at home, or elsewhere. The other occasions when you should also as a matter of routine check if your gun is loaded, we will deal with later.

Carrying a Gun

When you are merely walking with a gun, as opposed to holding it in readiness for a shot, you will want to carry it safely, and — subject to this — as conveniently and comfortably as you can. In order to achieve safety the muzzles must either point up in the air, or down at the ground clear of people's legs, dogs, etc. If you wish to have the muzzles pointing up in the air, the gun should be carried with the breech resting on the shoulder, so that the triggers and trigger guard are uppermost, and the hand should grip the stock in the region of the butt, as in *Diagram 45*. The stock should be kept well down, so that the barrels are almost vertical. There is one snag to this position; if you are walking alongside someone who is carrying his gun likewise, and one of you turns to look to a flank the barrels may come into collision, see *Diagram 46*. An alternative is to rest the butt on hip, and hold the stock by the hand, as in

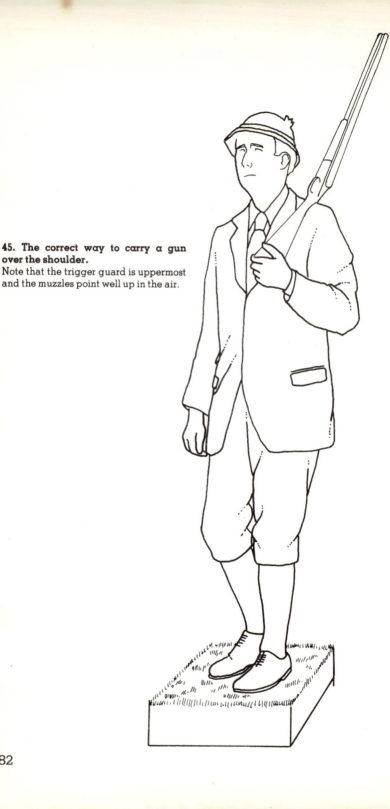

45. The correct way to carry a gun over the shoulder.
Note that the trigger guard is uppermost and the muzzles point well up in the air.

46. Danger of the barrels coming into collision when two people are walking side by side, each with his gun over the shoulder.

Diagram 47, which also allows the barrels to be kept nearly vertical. However it is not in my opinion such a comfortable position, nor quite so safe, because if you inadvertently stumble the muzzles

47. A gun can be safely carried with the butt resting on the hip.

are more liable to swing downwards and cover anyone in front of you.

To have the muzzles pointing at the ground, the gun is usually carried over the arm, as depicted in *Diagram 48a*. People sometimes hook their thumb in the front of their jacket to help take the weight; if you do so, beware of cocking up the muzzles so that they point at the legs of somebody in front. Many people like to enjoy a pipe or cigarette when out shooting; if you light up while walking along with the gun over your arm, the barrels will swing up into the horizontal (see *Diagram 49*) and point straight at a person in front, which is dangerous.

If you are walking down a steep incline you may find if you carry the gun on your shoulder that the man behind is looking down the muzzles, and if you place it over your arm they point at the back of the man in front; the answer in such circumstances is to carry the gun in the region of the middle of the fore-end with one hand so that the barrels are vertical, see *Diagram 50*, thus leaving your right hand free in case you slip.

If you are perforce carrying a loaded gun, such as when you are walking round a shoot on your own, it always seems to me that barrels pointing up in the air are safer than those pointing at the ground, i.e. one of the positions in *Diagrams 45* and *47* is to be preferred. If you are carrying an unloaded gun, it is good manners to do so with the breech open, so that other people can see at a glance that it is unloaded; in such circumstances it should be carried over the arm as in *Diagram 48b*.

This is all the novice needs to know at this juncture. I will elaborate on the above, and discuss ways in which guns should not be carried, in due course.

48. How to carry a gun over the arm with the breech closed, as in (a), or open, as in (b).

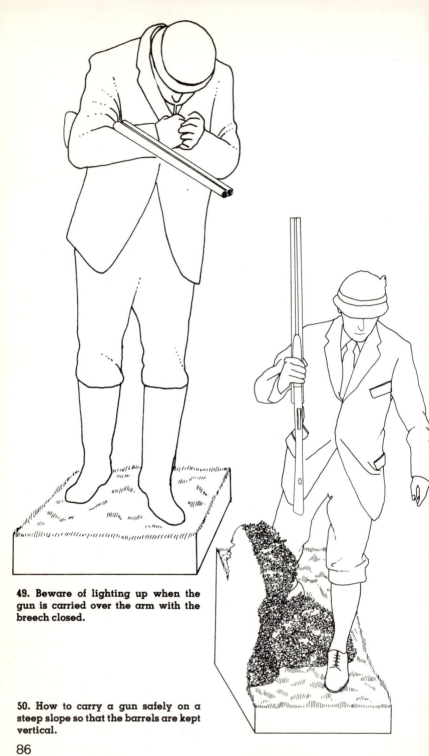

49. Beware of lighting up when the gun is carried over the arm with the breech closed.

50. How to carry a gun safely on a steep slope so that the barrels are kept vertical.

4   elements of marksmanship

General

In my experience few sportsmen have any knowledge of elementary optics, and therefore of how they can use their eyes to the fullest extent to help them in their shooting. As I have already indicated, successful game-shooting involves coordination of eyes and hands just as much as golf, cricket, or other such games. But because the target is hit by a charge of shot delivered via the gun barrels instead of directly by them, as in the case of a golf club or cricket bat, people are reluctant to trust their eyes to call their shots, and allow their hands to act naturally in concert with them. Among the first things a cricketer is taught are the importance of keeping his eye on the ball until he has completed his shot, and of making a positive stroke with his bat in order to hit it, because it has been found that simply to hold out the bat so that the ball does the striking is thoroughly unsatisfactory. If we apply these basic principles to our shooting, it should be clear that the shooter ought to:

a. Keep his eyes on the target until he has completed his shot.

b. Shoot at his target.

c. Make a positive movement with the gun as he brings it to the shoulder to take his shot, as if he intended to strike the target with the muzzles.

I believe that acceptance of these three points as the basis of your shooting technique is fundamental to the making of a marksman. If you 'poke' your gun around, firing at arbitrarily chosen points in space ahead of your targets, you are doing the equivalent of hanging your bat out to allow the ball to hit it, and as this necessitates taking your eye off the ball in mid-shot, any success you achieve with the gun is as much a fluke as in the case of a cricketer with his bat. But before we move on to see how our technique should be implemented in practice, there are one or two matters concerning the eyes, which it will help us in our shooting to know.

Simple Optics for Shooters

It is customary to use both eyes, because binocular vision enables us to judge distance and see in depth so that we can, for example, not only decide when a covey is within range, but also which is the nearest bird. It is perfectly possible to shoot with only one eye, but sportsmen who do so are handicapped in both these respects, though experience can to some extent alleviate the problem.

When you focus your eyes on a specific object, you retain a visual awareness of others within your field of vision, and the closer they are to the object of your attention, the greater this is.

It takes the eye a little while to re-focus on to an object close at hand from a distant one, and in general the older a person is, the longer it takes. So if you are waiting for game to be driven to you, it is a mistake to gaze intently at distant objects. You should look generally to your front at a distance of 50-60 yds, so that any movement within your field of vision will immediately catch your eye; this is especially applicable when you are shooting grouse or partridges in open country. When you anticipate a target appearing over a hedge or belt of trees, don't look at the hedge or tree tops, but into the 'blue' just above them. This can gain you an extra moment when quick shooting is required to deal with a target in front.

If you look at a linear object, your eyes will automatically fasten on the centre, unless you direct them specifically to another part of it. There are two aspects of this of particular interest to the shooter. As you mount your gun to the shoulder and the barrels enter your field of vision, your eyes will subconsciously register their centre-line, which should be that of the top rib if you are holding your gun correctly. It therefore follows that the more eye-catching the rib of your gun is, the easier the task of the eyes in this respect will be. So I believe that both the Churchill quick-sighting, tapered rib, and a raised flat file-cut rib, offer a definite advantage on this score over the traditional concave, game rib, especially when shooting in bad light conditions, as is often the case when wildfowling (see Ch. 2 and *Diagram 4*). It also appears to me to show that the advantage claimed for the 'single barrel sighting plane' of an over-and-under gun is more illusory than real. The second point the shooter should appreciate is that if the target has length, as does a cock pheasant or hare, your eyes will focus amidships, unless you direct them to the head. If you are shooting with a correctly fitting gun, and the actions of your eyes and hands in taking your shot are properly coordinated, the pattern will be centred exactly where you are looking. So failure to look in the right place, i.e. at the head, is often the reason why cock pheasants and hares are hit behind, instead of cleanly killed. The normal reaction of humans and animals on confrontation is to look each other in the eye, but in the case of gamebirds this is only practicable up to about 20 yds, as owing to the small size of their eye it is indistinguishable beyond this.

The Master Eye Theory

Most people have one arm, usually the right, stronger than the other, and such right-handed people are also generally stronger in their right leg than their left. It seems logical therefore to assume that their right eye will likewise be the stronger, or more dominant of the two. This is usually the case. If such a person is asked to look at something with one eye only, he will normally do so with the right, and close the left. But just as people differ in their degree of right-handedness, so too do they in that of their right-eye domin-ance. This is the basis of the 'Master Eye' theory used in gun fitting.

It is easy to find out which eye is the master by extending an arm and pointing the index finger at an object using both eyes. If you now close the left eye and your finger still appears aligned on the object, but when you open the left eye and close the right, it ap-pears to be pointing to the right of the object, then your right eye is the master. But just as some persons are as much at home using their left hand as their right, so some have eyes of equal strength, or what is known as centre vision.

Diagram 31 depicts an instance of someone whose right eye is completely the master. The greater the influence of the left eye, the more the centre-line of the barrels has to be moved over towards it, and hence the greater the amount of cast-off required on the stock. A shooting-coach, by using what is known as a 'try gun', that is one with an adjustable stock, can assess the amount of cast-off needed very accurately, but this should always be confirmed by shooting at a mark on the plate to make certain the pattern is really correctly centred.

Some people have in the past derided the 'master eye' theory, but I feel this may have been because they did not really understand it. It seems to me both simple and sound in practice, as I hope I have been able to explain.

Positioning and Use of the Eyes
The eyes are sometimes likened to the backsight of a rifle. I consider this is a bad analogy, because it suggests the presence of a foresight and the taking of an aim, as in rifle-shooting, which the shooter must NOT do. I therefore prefer to describe them as an optical sight motivating a computer, namely the brain, which activates the hands that direct the gun on to the target and fire it.

To do their job effectively the eyes must be correctly positioned in relation to the gun. When the shooter starts to bring his gun to the shoulder from the ready position, he should incline his head very slightly to the right. As he completes the movement he should bring the stock up to his cheek so that the line of the top of it comes to rest midway between cheekbone and jawbone, his eyes remaining level (see *Diagram 31* again). Some people, especially those who have first learned to shoot with a rifle, may tilt the head fractionally as they incline it to the right. The error thus induced is for practical purposes insignificant, but it is better to keep the head completely upright. However, it is a very different matter if the head is cocked over at the last moment to meet the stock, because the butt has not mounted high enough on the shoulder. In this case not only is your optical sight tilted markedly out of true level, but this has happened at the crucial moment just before firing, so an appreciable error of aim will occur. To obtain consistently satisfactory results the eyes must be in the same position in relation to the breech for each shot. The shooter will ensure this if he mounts his gun correctly, and remains 'stiff necked' until he has completed his shot.

Assuming you are in the ready position, let us now see what should happen as you take a shot at an incoming target. Having picked and fixed your eyes on the target, or in golfing parlance 'addressed it', your hands should instinctively direct your gun-muzzles on to it, and keep them there. Your eyes will now be making their assessment of target speed, range etc. The better the look you can allow them, the better the chance they have of doing their job effectively. There is no point in making a shot more difficult for yourself than it need be, so if you can be sure of a dead bird at 25-30 yds, don't risk a runner at 40 yds. As soon as your eyes tell you the moment has arrived to take your shot, start mounting the gun to your shoulder, as described in the previous chapter. As the barrels enter your field of vision, your eyes, although fixed on the target, will subconsciously align the top rib on it, and the moment the muzzles come to bear will give an order to the brain for the trigger to be pulled. Now if your hands have been acting properly in concert with your eyes, they will have been gradually accelerating the muzzles, so that at the moment your eyes said 'Shoot' these will have been overtaking the target. On receipt of the order, the brain activates the trigger finger, but the whole process is not instantaneous, and there is a brief interval between initiation by the eyes and completion by the trigger-finger, which is known as 'personal reaction time', and in a normally fit person is about a quarter of a second (0.25 sec.). During this interval the muzzles continue accelerating onwards, or 'overthrow'. This is equivalent to the 'follow through' of the head of a golf club or blade of a cricket bat after the ball has been struck, which in shooting is represented by the pulling of the trigger, the target being hit by the shot-charge during the 'overthrow' period. The full sequence of events is shown in *Diagram 51*. I hope all the foregoing has made clear that although it appeared to the shooter that he fired straight at his target, the overthrow induced by the impulsion imparted by his hands enabled the shot-charge to arrive at the right place to hit the target without any conscious estimating on his part.

Coordination of the Hands

When a batsman makes a scoring stroke at cricket and his timing is right, not only is the point of impact of bat and ball where he intended, but also coincides with that of maximum effort by his body in delivering the blow, the whole stroke being executed in one smoothly-flowing, incisive movement. The shooter should use his hands to mount the gun and fire it all in one similarly spontaneous, positive, uninterrupted movement, and if his timing is sound he too will score every time. If the appearance of a target takes us by surprise, we invariably react instinctively in this way, and our quarry generally falls dead. But when a bird, such as a driven pheasant, is seen approaching from afar, many people succumb to the temptation of bringing their gun to the shoulder prematurely, which

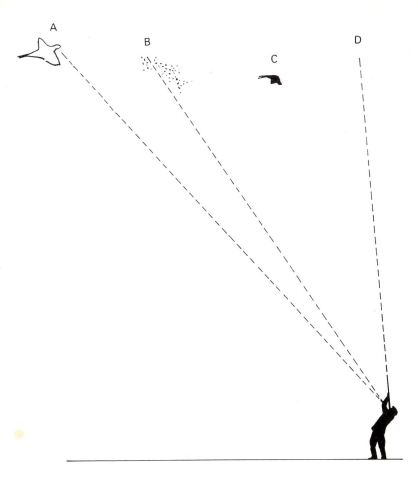

51. How 'Overthrow' works in practice.
'A' is the point at which the shooter's eye gave the order to fire. The
feathers in the air at 'B' indicate the point it had reached when hit
by the shot. 'C' is the dead bird falling, and 'D' is where the muzzles
were pointing as the shot was completed. This sequence was drawn
from a photograph taken at a shoot, and I hope the considerable
arc, 'A' — 'D', through which the barrels moved disposes of any idea
that this method is simply a form of snap shooting.

means they then have to make a pause, during which they often
take their eyes off the target for a quick squint along the barrels.
Finally they look back at their target, and swing the muzzles after it,
taking conscious aim. A miss behind is inevitable because by
pausing and breaking the rythm of their 'stroke' they have lost impulsion; also in checking their aim they have taken their eyes off the
'ball' and the final movement of the gun has been premeditated, not
spontaneous. The shooter must discipline himself to allow such
quarry to come almost within range before starting to move his gun

91

from the ready position, so that the shot can be completed in one movement. Only if this is done will the hands act instinctively in concert with the eyes, which are a very reliable instrument, and will feed the brain with all the information it needs to motivate the hands correctly, if we trust them.

It is often said that the killing of really high birds calls for very 'accurate' shooting, and that it is necessary to get well in front of them. Although this is in certain respects true, it is in my experience also very misleading. Let us see first what exactly is meant by 'accuracy'. Unhappily mention of this word in all kinds of shooting is always associated with aim. But in shotgun shooting it is more precisely a matter of centring the charge correctly, which if we have a properly fitting gun, depends on mounting the butt to the right place on the shoulder. I have already explained that although the effective spread of our pattern covers a 30-in. circle, this is insufficient to compensate for even quite small errors in gun-fitting, and that an error of this kind can be induced by the butt being bedded home incorrectly at the shoulder. As far as the game-shooter is concerned 'accuracy' is therefore primarily a matter of polished gun-mounting, and nothing to do with aiming as such.

As regards the need to 'get well in front of high birds', I would stress again that it is just as much a mistake to start shooting at points in space ahead of such targets, as with those nearer at hand. If the shooter allows high birds to come well in, looks at the head, and trusts his eyes, his hands will provide all the impulsion needed to induce the required overthrow. However, they are a special kind of shot, so experience and practice are necessary to enable a shooter to deal with them with the same facility as other targets.

Everyone who is learning to shoot will sooner or later hear somebody talk about the need for 'swing', and how you can't hope to shoot successfully without it. If we look again at *Diagram 51*, it will be seen that the trigger was pulled when the barrels were pointing at **A**, the bird struck by the shot at **B** and the barrels have ended up pointing at **D**. They have thus swung through an arc of 40°, without taking into account any movement before the trigger was pulled. As this drawing was taken from a photograph this is an example of what happens in practice, and not mere theory. I hope this amply illustrates that if you allow the hands to act instinctively in concert with eyes, the impulsion they impart takes care of 'swing' and the shooter has no need to worry about it.

Personal Reaction Time

In recent years a comprehensive study has been made of the phenomenon known as personal reaction-time, because of its importance in connection with the development of safety techniques in flying high-speed aircraft. This has revealed that if a person is confronted with an emergency for which he is unprepared, it will take him about 0.75 seconds to react. If however he is already alerted, as is the shooter when he is about to pull the trigger, it will take him less than half as long to do so. So a shooter's personal reaction-time can be reckoned at between 0.25 and 0.35 seconds. This time varies quite extensively from person to person, and with a given person according to his physical and mental state. Thus, to shoot at his best a sportsman needs to be physically and mentally fit. Tiredness in one or both respects can cause temporary loss of form, as many rough-shooters have probably found to their cost towards the end of a long, arduous day. Smoking, and the consumption of food and alcohol, also exert an influence which may be beneficial or detrimental, as the case may be. However, I believe we all have a built-in capacity to compensate for minor fluctuations in our personal reaction-time, and it is only if we have really overdone things that we experience a problem in this respect.

There are two other time factors involved before the shot charge reaches the target, which may be mentioned appropriately at this juncture. They are time up the barrel, and time of flight. The former, including time of ignition, i.e. the fall of the tumbler, has been estimated to be 0.0056 seconds. With a standard-velocity cartridge and No.6 shot, the time of flight to a target at 40 yds is 0.14 seconds, or roughly half the personal reaction-time. However, it is of course less at shorter ranges. I believe that as a shooter gains experience, so does he automatically make allowance for this, and need not worry about it.

There is one further aspect of timing in shooting that is little appreciated. If a cricketer is faced with a change of bowling, he has a good look at the first few balls from the new bowler so that his eyes can adjust to the different pace, flight etc. Yet a sportsman who has settled into the rhythm needed to deal successfully with a certain kind of target is often thrown completely out of his stride by the appearance of a different shot. We have all probably suffered at some time from red faces after missing embarassingly easy shots in such circumstances. This is simply because we have failed to take account of the change of 'bowling' and paused to allow our eyes a really good look to register the difference in the new target before taking our shot. The pace and behaviour of all our quarry differ. The rough-shooter usually has no difficulty in adjusting to each as he encounters them, because their variety prohibits the development of a set rhythm in his shooting. But those who go to shoot, say, driven grouse, and then later turn to driven pheasants, should not be surprised if at first they are a little off form in dealing with the latter, for reasons which I will deal with more fully later.

Conclusion

Game shooting always used to be considered a sport at which you could not shine unless you were specially gifted because it required a unique and inexplicable technique to master the art of good marksmanship. In my view this is nonsense. Any reasonably competent games player ought to be able to become as good a shot as his natural ability to coordinate the actions of his eyes and hands allows, if he carries out the drill I have set out in this and previous chapters. But as in all games and sports mastery will be obtained only with practice, and unless a novice is prepared to devote time and effort to this, preferably under the guidance of a qualified instructor at a shooting-school, he will never be able to shoot at his best, and so do full justice to the quarry he pursues.

5 special considerations for young shots

Making a Start

There are certain legal restrictions on the use of shotguns by young persons, which are explained later in this chapter. Every parent of an aspiring young shot should be aware of these and see that his offspring also is. But apart from the limitations thereby imposed, the age at which a young person can start learning to handle and shoot with a shotgun remains at a parent's discretion. Opinions differ quite considerably as to what this age should be. It seems to me that the criterion ought to be that the young person in question has not only the physical capacity to handle a gun competently but also the mental maturity to appreciate that even a small-bore gun, such as a .410, is a potentially lethal weapon which must at all times be carried, handled, and used safely. I believe therefore that as a rule 10 years of age is quite early enough to start teaching elementary gun handling, and 12 for actual shooting. However there will of course be exceptions, and some may be able to make a start rather sooner, while others will need to wait a year or so longer. But as soon as a boy or girl begins taking a genuine interest in shooting, and to enjoy accompanying an adult on a walk round with gun and dog, it is never too early to start inculcating the basic rules of safety, which are set out in the next chapter. In this connection it is however important to ensure that whoever they accompany is likely to set them a good and not a bad example in such matters. Young people are naturally observant and imitative, and so just as likely to pick up bad habits as good, until they know better. So a parent should either undertake this initial tuition himself, or see that it is done by someone whom he knows is an experienced shot. If properly arranged in this way, the aspiring novice will gain valuable experience in the ways and etiquette of the shooting-field, which will give him a flying start when he first goes out with a gun of his own.

Overgunning and Undergunning

When the time comes to select a first gun for a boy or girl, great stress is always laid upon the dangers of over-gunning, i.e. of having a gun which is of too big a gauge and fires too heavy a charge. This is quite right, because if recoil is too severe, it may cause painful bruising of the cheek and shoulder, and thus induce various faults in shooting technique, such as lifting the cheek off the stock, which will prejudice success and later prove difficult to cure.

It may even discourage a youngster from shooting altogether. Only rarely does the converse problem of under-gunning receive any attention. This is wrong. Smaller loads mean less shot, with consequently reduced pattern densities, and therefore shorter effective ranges, which make it more difficult to obtain successful results, as explained in Chapter 2. In the case of the .410, the $2\frac{1}{2}$-in. cartridge has a shot-load of $\frac{7}{16}$ oz., which gives a total of 149 pellets of No.7 shot. For small quarry such as woodpigeon, grey squirrels etc., a minimum pattern-density of 130 pellets in the 30-in. circle is required (see Table 6), which is 87 per cent of the total charge. With an improved-cylinder barrel this percentage pattern can be obtained only up to a range of about 23 yds, though with a full choke it should be obtainable up to just under 35 yds, (see Table 11). However I have discovered, as have others, that .410 barrels of all borings tend to shoot patterns of below-par density, and the greater the degree of choke, the more pronounced this failing becomes, so that for practical purposes 20 yds must be considered the maximum effective range of a .410 improved-cylinder barrel with a $2\frac{1}{2}$-in. load of No.7 shot, and 25 yds that of a full-choke barrel with this load. These limits are very restricting even for shooting at clays, and if exceeded with live quarry only aggravate the chance of wounding, which is something to be avoided at all costs. In learning any game or sport nothing gives a novice greater encouragement than success, and this is just as true of shooting. I believe therefore that a .410 is a bad gun with which to launch a young person on his or her shooting career because it limits so severely the chances of achieving reasonable success.

A far better proposition is the 28-bore. The standard load is $\frac{9}{16}$ oz. of shot. A double-barrelled gun of this bore weighing about 5 lb. should not be too heavy for even a rather slender youngster of 12 years of age to handle comfortably, nor should the recoil be excessive. These guns also offer certain definite advantages. They are of standard boxlock or sidelock construction, so that a novice can learn right from the start the correct procedures for loading, unloading, putting off the safety-catch, etc. They shoot patterns true to form, so that an improved-cylinder barrel with No.7 shot will produce patterns of sufficient density to kill small quarry cleanly up to 30 yds, and a half-choke barrel up to 35 yds. These are not only much more practical limits, but are achieved with 'game borings'. These little guns give a young person a real chance to shoot well at clays, and obtain a lot of good sport dealing with small pests and predators under the eye of an adult.

Gun Fitting

A mistake often made is to start a young person with a gun too long in the stock for him, because he will soon grow into it and it spoils the look of a gun to shorten the stock and then lengthen it again. The importance of correct stock-length generally has been dealt with in Chapter 3, but it is absolutely vital in the case of a first gun.

52. The disastrous consequences of starting a Young Shot with a gun too long in the stock.
The faults noted will be aggravated if the gun is also too heavy.

Unless his stock is the correct length a young shot will not be able to hold the gun correctly or mount it properly to his shoulder; in consequence he will have to adapt his stance and otherwise fit himself to it in order to shoot. What will happen with too long a stock is shown in *Diagram 52*, which I hope makes quite clear how this fault utterly prohibits the aspiring shooter from adopting the right technique.

After a stock has been cut down to the right size initially, it will subsequently need to be lengthened as the young shooter grows, to maintain the fit. A competent gunsmith should be able to do this at comparatively little cost.

Although bend and cast-off should be checked for a first gun, and any necessary adjustments made, in the majority of cases these are of much less consequence until a person starts to broaden out in his late teens.

The Law and Young Shots

Under the law relating to Shotgun Certificates, it is illegal to sell, lend, or give a shotgun to anyone who is not the holder of a valid shotgun certificate; a shotgun may not be given to anyone under 15 years of age. The effect of this is that if, for example, a parent borrows a shotgun from a friend for the use of his 13-year-old son during a school holiday, he himself must possess a valid shotgun certificate.

The issue of shotgun certificates to young persons under the age of 15 years is not debarred, but may be effected at the discretion of the Chief Police Officer to whom application is made. No minimum age at which a certificate is issuable has been laid down, so the decision rests entirely with the Chief Police Officer concerned, and the views of some as to what is a suitable age may differ from others.

A shotgun certificate is not needed if:

a. A shotgun is borrowed from the occupier of private premises including land, and used thereon in his presence.

b. Someone else's shotgun is used on artificial targets at a place and time approved by the local Chief Police Officer, e.g. at an established shooting-ground.

There are other exemptions, but they are not especially applicable to young shots. However, certain clauses of the Firearms Acts 1937 and 1965, and the Airguns and Shotguns Act 1962 are relevant.

No one under 14 years of age may possess, purchase, or acquire any firearm or ammunition, nor may he be lent any such weapon or ammunition. But he may:

a. Possess and use firearms and ammunition as a member of an approved club, or when shooting in a shooting-gallery where only air weapons or miniature rifles are available.

b. Carry a firearm or ammunition under the instruction of another person over 21, who holds a valid shotgun or firearms certificate relating to the weapon or ammunition in question.

If a person is under 15 years of age and has a shotgun certificate, he may have an assembled shotgun with him provided that he is supervised by a person over 21 or the shotgun is carried in a cover securely fastened. When he is 15 or over, and has a shotgun certificate, he may be given a shotgun as a gift.

Until a person is 17 years of age he may not purchase or hire any firearm or its ammunition. But on reaching this age, provided he has a shotgun certificate, he may possess, purchase, acquire, and use a shotgun and its ammunition subject only to the current legal restrictions applicable in these respects to adults.

This is the substance of the law as I understand it. But I am not a lawyer, and anyone who has any doubts or queries on the above, or other matters relating to young shots, should consult a qualified solicitor.

Initial Shooting Lessons

Many people shoot for years without ever seeing the patterns shot by a gun, and consequently have only the haziest idea of what these look like. I like therefore at the start of his first lesson to show a young shot these either on a whitwashed plate, or on a paper target 5ft × 5ft at ranges of 20 and 30 yds respectively, assuming he has a 28-bore. A circle of 15-in radius can then be described round the centre of the pattern in each case, which will enable him to see for himself the effective spread. It should be stressed that although the effective range of a 28-bore is only 30 - 35 yds, the individual pellets may carry on for over 200 yds before they become spent, and so may inflict injury on anyone up to that range.

Clay targets should be used for these initial lessons, in which the aim should be to build up a shooter's self-confidence. So I make a start with five clays set up on edge in a line on the ground and spaced a yard apart. As soon as these are 'killed' with a shot apiece at 25 yds, starting 'gun down', it will be time enough to progress to moving targets. For these either a hand-thrower or a trap with the spring slackened off can be used to project a well lobbed-up going-away bird. When this has been mastered, easy incoming birds can be introduced, but somebody else will be needed to operate the trap or thrower from behind suitable cover, so that the 'instructor' is free to stand with and keep an eye on his pupil.

These early lessons should be kept short; 25 - 30 cartridges is probably quite enough, and always try to end them with a 'kill'. More varied, difficult, and challenging birds can then be introduced as the pupil's progress dictates, until the great day arrives when he has sufficiently mastered the art of shooting to try for a rabbit, woodpigeon, or grey squirrel.

6 safety in the shooting field

The Most Important Qualification of All

When you have begun to master the elements of marksmanship by shooting clays, you will be eager to try your skill in the field. But before you do so, you must fully appreciate the need always to shoot safely, even if this means on occasions refraining from discharging your gun at all. The supreme ambition of every shooting man should be to earn himself a reputation as a safe shot. If he can combine this with one as a first-class marksman also, good luck to him, but it should be of only secondary concern. I propose therefore to deal with safety in the shooting-field before tackling the problems of marksmanship various gamebirds and other quarry may pose, so that these latter can be considered in perspective against the background of the former.

The Twin Aspects of Safety

If you have been properly taught you will have already learned some basic rules of safe gun-handling (*see* pp. 81-86). You may, or may not, also have had pointed out to you, or realised for yourself, that shooting with a mechanically sound gun using a properly matched cartridge makes an equally important contribution to safety, (*see* Chapter 2). A well-maintained gun should be a mechanically reliable one, just as should a properly cared-for car. Likewise, when you buy a gun, you will obtain basically what you pay for. So if you acquire a cheap one, you cannot expect 'Rolls Royce' handling and performance. You may hear some folk talk disparagingly of 'best' guns, and say that you are only paying for a 'name' and some fancy engraving. Such nonsense is best ignored. A 'Best' gun is made from the finest materials by the most skilled craftsmen, to give first-class handling and shooting qualities. But a best gun is as much beyond the pockets of many of us as a Rolls Royce car, and just as there are other cars that will give excellent service and satisfactory performance for a lesser price, so there are many guns that will provide the same. However, again as in the case of a car, it is worth spending as much as you can afford on a gun, because the better its quality, the greater its built-in margin of safety. If a sound-quality gun is properly looked after by its owner, he should be able to enjoy a lifetime of good sport with it. However, even the best guns will exceptionally suffer a mechanical breakdown in the field. In over 35 years such a misfortune has only overtaken me once, when a mainspring broke, and many sportsmen never experience a mishap of this kind in their whole careers. Incidents of this sort are a very different matter from mechanical failure due to lack of maintenance, a typical example of which is when the nose of the sear does not engage properly in the bent on cocking, and causes a premature discharge of the cartridge. In two instances of this which have come to my notice, one was due to the lock having become clogged with old oil and dirt, or in plain words lack of maintenance, and the other to excessive wear of the sear-nose because of its inferior metal. Both these instances could have proved dangerous if the gun in each case had not discharged itself into soft ground. I hope this highlights the very real contribution both maintenance and quality make to the mechanical safety of a gun.

The Rules of Safety

Safe gun-handling and shooting in the field are in the main a matter of following established drills, but there is no substitute for everyday commonsense in applying these to special situations which can and do arise, but which are not specifically mentioned. The principal contingencies are covered by the following rules:

1. Prove if a gun is loaded or not as soon as you lay hands on it.
2. Only point a gun at quarry you wish to shoot, *never* at people.
3. Check that the bore(s) of your barrel(s) is/are clear before you load at the beginning of a day, drive, walk up, or after any appreciable interval between shots, and invariably after a misfire.
4. Never put down or leave a loaded gun.
5. Carry a gun with the barrels pointing either up in the air or down at the ground, except when you come to the ready position, when they should point where you are looking.
6. Learn to shoot in good style; polished performance promotes safety.
7. Don't shoot where you cannot see; small shot can travel up to about 250 yds before it becomes spent, and may ricochet off stones, hard ground, water, or the branches of trees, etc.
8. Always check that your gun is unloaded before crossing an obstacle, or entering a car or building.
9. Don't be a greedy shot; observe proper safety angles, (see *Diagram 54*), never swing your muzzles through the line of guns or beaters, or any individual, such as a stop.
10. Use only cartridges which you know give ballistics within the limits for which your gun has passed Proof.
11. If you take a dog shooting with you, make sure it is always kept under proper control, and does not have to be attached by a lead to your person to this end.
12. Don't take other people on trust as safe shots; make it your business to find out for yourself.

Let us now examine the practical implications of these rules. I have already dealt at some length in Chapter 7 with the need to 'prove' whether or not a firearm of any description is loaded as soon as you pick it up. I will therefore only add that this to my mind is the crucial test, and anyone who fails to pass it is not to be trusted as a safe shot.

Without, I hope, sounding like an Old Testament prophet relishing another opportunity to play the part of a harbinger of doom, the number of people to be seen nowadays at shoots waving their gun around like a flagpole, pointing the muzzles indiscriminately at other people and their dogs, is absolutely terrifying. Not so long ago such behaviour would have prompted a sharp rebuke from the host, or a fellow sportsman, and rightly so. The verse from Mark Beaufoy's *A Father's Advice*:

> Never, never let your gun,
> Pointed be at anyone;
> That it may unloaded be,
> Matters not the least to me

should be scrupulously observed by everyone carrying a gun in the shooting-field at all times. Obviously in running a syndicate it is desirable to strike a happy balance between efficiency and officiousness. But where safe gun-handling is concerned, the line between what is permissible and what is not must be tightly drawn, because slackness feeds on itself, and where allowed to go by default will inevitably lead to the occurance of an accident sooner or later. In a good syndicate the observance of elementary safety-rules should be as much the responsibility of every member as the person appointed to run its affairs. Where this is so, a timely tactful word should suffice to correct any lapse, and keep matters on a sound and happy basis, even when a guest gun poses the problem. Occasionally prompt and more forceful action may need to be taken, and when this arises the fact that the offender has paid for his gun in the syndicate should not be allowed to inhibit such action being taken. To quote again from *A Father's Advice*:

> You may kill or you may miss,
> But at all times think of this;
> All the pheasants ever bred,
> Won't repay for one man dead.

Always checking that the bores of the barrels are clear before loading, as outlined in Rule 3, may seem a trifle over-cautious. But it is amazing how pieces of mud, bits of tow or cleaning rag and other small items of debris, can manage to lodge themselves there. Only a comparatively slight obstruction of the bore is necessary to cause a bulged or burst barrel. Once when shooting pigeon from a hide I returned after tidying up the decoys, and on inspecting the bores discovered some feathers had mysteriously inserted themselves half way down one of them. On another occasion having walked through long frost-covered grass with my gun over my arm, I found quite a thick layer of ice had built up in the chokes. So this precaution is an essential one, and every shooter should train himself to perform it instinctively. I always carry a pulthrough with a bristle brush on the end in case an obstruction cannot be shaken or blown out; it has only had to be used once for my own gun, but on several occasions for those of others when the muzzles have become clogged with mud due to a mishap.

The reason for inspecting the bore in addition to the breech after a misfire is the possibility that a cartridge of smaller gauge may have been loaded in error, and then slipped forward and lodged in the cone of the chamber. This can happen if a 20-bore cartridge is loaded by mistake into a 12-bore, or a 28-bore one into a 16-bore. If such a cartridge then lodges in the cone, it is possible to load one of correct gauge on top of it, so that the gun is double-shotted. If the gun is now fired the pressure generated by the explosion of both cartridges is usually fierce enough to crack the action right through in the line of the face, and rip the barrel asunder for a substantial distance in front of the breech. It may well cause the shooter the loss of one or more fingers, possibly an eye, or some other serious injury. So if you ever have a misfire, and such is the reliability of modern British cartridges that this is a very rare contingency with a properly maintained gun, always check that the bore, not merely the chamber, is clear before you reload.

To round off this question of misfires; if on opening the breech after one there is a normal cartridge of correct gauge in the chamber, you should inspect the cap to ascertain if it has been properly struck. If it appears to have been so, the fault may lie with the cartridge. But the great majority of straightforward misfires nowadays are due to a fault in the gun, not the cartridge; and where two or more instances of misfiring occur with different cartridges, this will almost invariably prove the case. I would stress this because the instinctive reaction of many people is to blame the cartridge, and as a result they continue to suffer from misfires when probably what is required to remedy the situation is some quite minor repair or adjustment to their gun.

The validity of Rule 4 may seem so indisputable that it is pointless to elaborate on it. But loaded guns are still put down and left by their owners so that they are subsequently knocked down or for some other reason come to be fired accidentally. I have seen a loaded gun, bearing the name of a most reputable maker, placed on the ground at it's owner's feet so that he could light a cigarette. While he was doing so one barrel discharged itself, narrowly missing his dog sitting in front of him, and considerably alarming a stop standing 50 yds away at the corner of the covert, but fortunately out of the direct line of fire. Quite rightly the person concerned gave up shooting for the day, and sent his gun to be put in order. But although he had always otherwise shown himself to be a careful shot, it took him a whole season to regain his reputation as such among the beaters on that shoot. However 'safe' it may appear to make an exception to the rules, it is always tempting providence to do so, and if you wish to maintain a reputation as a safe shot, it is simply not worth the risk.

The basic ways in which you should carry a gun (Rule 5) have been discussed in Chapter 7. There are of course ways other than those described in which a gun can be safely carried, but in my opinion the two depicted in *Diagram 53a and b* should not be employed, because although it is possible to keep the muzzles elevated at a safe angle, the tendency is for them to droop so that they don't remain so.

Some controversy exists over when it is not only good manners but good sense to carry your gun with the breech open, to show that it is unloaded. As a guideline, it is in my view right so to carry it when you do not anticipate having to take a shot, and are in the company of others who could in the circumstances be justified in thinking it might be loaded — for example when you join your companions at the end of a drive, or if you approach a fellow gun at the beginning of a drive to pass on or obtain information. Some people say that a gun is more liable to suffer damage if it is carried with the breech open. This is true in certain circumstances, such as when one is crossing rough ground especially on a hillside or steep bank. But occasions like these are rare on a normal day's rough or covert shooting, and seem to me merely the exceptions that prove the rule. If a shooting-man relies on his commonsense he will very soon be able to judge exactly when it is, and is not, appropriate to carry his gun with the breech open. To try and be any more dogmatic, as certain contributors to the correspondence columns of the sporting Press sometimes are, seems to me silly.

Some shoots make it a rule that at the end of each drive, when everyone has unloaded, each person places his gun in a canvas or leather cover and carries it in this until he reaches his stand for the next drive. This is a very sound practice. In particular it removes any temptation to take pot shots at birds subsequently flushed by dogs picking up, which can be extremely dangerous and should be firmly suppressed.

If you watch an accomplished shot in a hot corner, you will see him mount, fire, and reload his gun, pick his next target, and repeat the process again and again, all in a fluent routine, conspicuously devoid of any signs of undue haste or 'flap'. He will seem to know instinctively where his safe arcs-of-fire are, and not waste a second glance at birds outside them, however tempting a shot they may offer. It is a pleasure, as well as instructive, to watch the performance of such an expert. He will have spent the spare time at the beginning of the drive working out where it will and will not be safe to shoot when the birds start to come forward, and where if practicable he will try to kill them. He will have made sure he has as clear and level a platform as the ground allows so that he can use his feet to full advantage, and that his cartridges are as conveniently disposed as possible to assist in quick reloading. Experience will have taught him those targets which give him a genuine chance of being able to

53. Two potentially unsafe ways of carrying a gun.
Although the muzzles can be kept safely elevated, there is a marked
tendency for them to droop and point at anyone on the shooter's left.

reload in time to deal with them and those which do not, and so can
be ignored. In consequence, he always appears to have just that little bit of extra time in hand which enables him to judge whether or
not an unexpected opportunity is a safe shot, whereas the novice in
such circumstances may get in such a state of fluster that safety
either becomes a matter of good luck rather than good judgement,
or he hardly lets his gun off at all. There are good, safe shots who
lack the advantage of good style. I say this advisedly, because they
have managed to become so despite their lack of style, not because
of it. So be in no doubt that polished performance does promote
safety, as well as lending distinction to your shooting.

Don't shoot where you cannot see (Rule 7); probably more accidents occur in the field from failure to observe this rule than any
other, for although the maximum *effective* range of a 12-bore is only
around 45 yds, and that of a 28-bore about 10 yds less, individual
pellets of small shot (i.e. 5s, 6s, or 7s) carry on to approximately 250
yds before they become spent, irrespective of the gauge of gun from

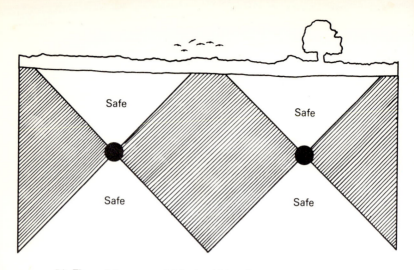

54. The safety zones which should be observed in the shooting field in relation to other people.

which they have been fired, and those of larger shot to an even greater distance. Even at a range of 150 yds a pellet may have sufficient remaining energy to blind someone for life if it hits him in the eye, quite apart from the danger of ricochets. Comparatively few shooting-men appreciate what a danger this latter can be. Because of their small size, spherical shape, and relatively low velocity, shot pellets will ricochet off any reasonably hard surface, such as the branches of trees, even the quills of gamebird feathers, as well as the surface of water, stones and frozen ground. Although the safety zones which should be observed (*Diagram 54*), take account of all the possibilities that may be reasonably anticipated, the angle through which a pellet may be deflected on ricochet is wholly unpredictable and instances have been known where it has been as much as 135°. Fortunately such freak occurrences are extremely rare indeed, and for the purpose of assessing practical danger areas can be discounted.

Special care should be taken when shooting ground game — i.e. hares and rabbits — in cover or alongside hedgerows. If you cannot see whether you have a clear field of fire the other side of any cover whatsoever, don't shoot. The same applies to any low-flying winged game, be it a pheasant flying back along the line of a hedge, or a covey of partridges scudding away low over roots towards a hedge, a much prized woodcock, or even that carrion crow you have been trying to get to terms with for weeks, don't shoot where you cannot see, irrespective of whether you are having a walk round on your own or shooting in the company of others.

As regards Rule 8, the danger of bringing a loaded shotgun into a dwelling, for example, seems patently obvious. Yet despite this, fatal accidents are reported in the daily Press every year due to failure to observe this apparently self-evident precaution.

It is a pleasure to see anyone making the most of his chances, especially when game is scarce. It can be extremely irritating in such circumstances if you, yourself, are shooting well, to have to watch your neighbour miss handsomely with both barrels time and time again, and it becomes very tempting to try to do his work for him. But it is a temptation that should be resisted, because it very easily becomes a habit. Nothing is more exasperating when you are awaiting a shot at a bird heading straight for you than to find that it arrives dead at your feet, because your neighbour has shot it for you. Your instinctive reaction will be to retaliate in kind, but this sort of competitive shooting can very quickly deteriorate into dangerous shooting, and although it may initially be done purely in fun, can soon develop into something more serious. This kind of situation can arise between good shots, who should know better, but whatever the circumstances the host or person in charge should put a stop to it.

When walking up snipe it is accepted that as soon as a bird flushes anyone within range may shoot at it. Otherwise if any quarry rises in front of a gun or is coming straight to him, it is considered good manners to allow him first shot at it, and only if he misses should his neighbour have a try at 'wiping his eye', as it is known.

If, having killed or missed in front, you wish to turn to take a shot behind, you should bring the stock down from your shoulder so that the muzzles point up in the air as the gun swings past other people in the line; then as you complete your turn remount the gun to your shoulder and shoot. This drill should be observed even if only a single person, maybe even a spectator, is involved. The correct sequence is shown in *Diagram 55*.

The importance of using only cartridges which give ballistics within the limits for which your gun has been proved (Rule 10) has already been dealt with in Chapter 2. British cartridges have marked on the box the guns for which they are suitable. With some brands of foreign cartridges this is not always clear; in any case of doubt, it is advisable to consult a qualified gunsmith before using them, or you may damage both your gun and yourself.

For many shooting-men much of the pleasure they derive from their sport stems from handling and working their dog. This is fine provided the dog in question is steady and a competent performer. A dog that is neither is more than merely a nuisance, it is a potential menace. In particular I dislike seeing people out shooting with a dog attached by a lead to their belt. If a sizeable dog of any breed plunges forward just as its owner is about to shoot, the latter may be thrown off balance, and the charge go anywhere. So if you want to shoot with a dog, which to my mind is more than half the fun of the game, make sure it is properly trained, and steady to fur and feather, so that you take *it* shooting, and it does not take you.

It is always pleasant to be in a position to be able to invite a guest

to a day's shooting. But I would strongly recommend that if you have no firsthand knowledge of whether or not he (or she) is a safe and experienced shot, you take steps to find out before issuing the invitation. Otherwise you can find yourself in the embarrassing position of having a complete tyro on your hands, who is attending his first formal shoot, hasn't the faintest idea what to do, and handles his gun with a carefree abandon that frightens the living daylights out of everyone. I was once badly caught out in this way myself, and have subsequently witnessed the discomfiture of others on more than one occasion. Although such situations may be the stuff of splendid after-dinner stories, they are seldom so funny to those directly involved at the time.

These are the basic safety 'drills' that every aspiring sportsman should mark, learn, and perfect if he is to become a safe shot and enjoy a reputation as one. There is of course a great deal more in the way of etiquette that will be learned from experience. Two important aspects of this are that the word of one's host, or whoever is in charge of a day's shooting, is law, and that game-shooting is an enjoyable recreation only so long as it is conducted safely. As far as this latter aspect is concerned, everyone, not only the host or manager of a shoot, has a vested interest in seeing that the code of safety is observed, and if necessary enforced.

55. Correct gun-handling when turning to take a shot behind.
Note that the stock has been lowered from the shoulder after the firing of the first barrel in front so that the muzzles point safely upwards as the turn is made.

7 game shooting

Making Ready

As mentioned in the previous chapter, one of the distinguishing characteristics of an experienced shot is that even in a hot corner he always seems to retain his composure. An important contribution to this happy state of affairs is the use he makes of his time at the beginning of a drive to prepare for such an eventuality. The following routine is suggested as a guide to what may be done in this respect:

1. Select exactly where you wish to stand to shoot. If you are on rough ground or a ploughed field, tread as level a platform as you can, making sure it is sufficiently large to allow you to turn freely. Clear any loose debris such as sticks or stones which may otherwise impede the movement of your feet; on a root field it is normally permissible to pull the odd plant or two for this purpose.

2. Sit your dog where you want him. Whether this is in front of you, to one side, or behind you, make sure he is well clear of your feet, as also his lead if you have him on one attached to a peg in the ground. If a dog jumps up and pulls his lead tight, it can become an all too effective tripwire.

3. Place your cartridge-bag where it will be easily accessible and, if on the ground, also well clear of your feet. If the weather is fine the flap can be turned back. See that your 'ready to use' supply in your coat pocket or cartridge-belt is in order.

4. Plant your shooting-seat where you want it, just in rear of your 'platform', and place any other kit — e.g. your gun sleeve, etc. — on the ground behind it.

5. Having checked that the bores are clear, load your gun.

6. Check where your neighbouring guns are. If it is not obvious, as may sometimes be the case in woodland or other cover, make sure they also know where you are.

7. Check where any stops/flankers are positioned, and also any pickers-up who may be standing back. If you have been told a stop or flanker will move to a certain place in the course of a drive make a mental note of it. Pickers-up may sometimes be delayed at the previous drive and arrive late, so allow for this where applicable.

8. Work out your safe arcs of fire; where practicable choose prominent landmarks, e.g. the corner of a wood, a lone tree in a hedge, or the chimney of a cottage, to indicate these. (N.B. It is inadvisable to use stationary farm implements as markers, because however unlikely it may seem, they may be moved during the

critical period you are relying on them remaining in position.)

9. Estimate the limit of effective range (i.e. 40 yds) within your safe arcs of fire. This is more obviously important on a grouse moor and when shooting partridges or hares over open downland than at a covert shoot. However, even in this latter type of shooting it is always useful to have an idea of the range to the covert's edge. I also like to have a mental picture of a datum line drawn across the front edge of a wood below which no birds are to be shot on grounds of both safety and ethics.

10. Finally, just as a golfer often likes to limber up by having a couple of practice swings before addressing the ball, so a shooter may profit from mounting his gun once or twice at an imaginary target to make sure the butt comes cleanly and correctly to his shoulder.

11. If you have a picker-up standing with you, he will normally position himself and his dog(s) just behind you, and out of your way. But if you have any special views of your own as to where you want him to stand, you may of course ask him to conform to them.

Having completed this sequence, or such part of it as is applicable, a shooter can relax on his shooting-seat to await the approach of the quarry. During this interval you should remain alert but relaxed, and look generally towards the covert or into the 'blue' just over the top of it. This will enable you to detect any movement of game coming forward within your field of vision, and then focus your eyes on it, as explained in Chapter 4. Birds flushed early in a beat sometimes escape unscathed because the gun concerned has allowed his attention to wander, and is caught napping. If this happens don't become tensed up and over-anxious to redeem your lapse. If you do, you will probably start trying to 'make sure' of your next shot, mount your gun prematurely and miss. This will add to your state of tension, and probably prove the start of a series of misses, which for an inexperienced shot can be a disastrous beginning to a day's sport from which he may never recover. Imperturbability is just as important a quality in the make-up of a good shot, as is self-confidence. In game-shooting, as in other games and sports, a good start is of course the finest stimulant to the latter you can have. Thus I always try to make the first shot of the day as easy as I can for myself by allowing my quarry to come well in so that if possible I am virtually looking it 'in the eye' as I shoot. To the same end, I seek to avoid a 'spectacular', i.e. a borderline chance, for which plenty of opportunities will most likely arise later, when one has got one's eye in. This, to my mind, is merely sensible gamesmanship. It should not be confused with another phenomenon, namely, the habit of some people of not taking certain shots at which they know they are weak although the target is well within range. To a host who can only show his guests a limited number of birds this can be a very annoying trait, and I know of one instant where a culprit was in consequence never invited again.

It is disconcerting to be told, possibly a trifle brusquely, at the end of a drive, 'Oh, we aren't shooting such-and-such to-day', when in all innocence you have just done so. Even the best of managers may forget to tell a guest making his first appearance what the form is in this respect. So if you are not told at the meet, it is always wise to enquire what may, and may not be shot, so as to save yourself any subsequent embarrassment.

Concerning Cartridges

When attending a shoot for the first time, you should ascertain how many cartridges you are likely to need. In my experience the answer you receive will often err on the low side. On the basis that it is better to have too many than too few, I invariably take substantially more than I am told or anticipate will be required. This is especially important if you shoot with a 16-bore or 20-bore, because when you are the only person with a gun of such a gauge nobody will be able to come to your rescue if your own supply fails. For many shoots a full bag of 100 will suffice, but I always like to have a second full bag of the same size in reserve. If you are bidden to shoot wood-pigeon, either over decoys or flighting into roost, you can never tell what fortune may bring. If, in addition to a full bag of 100, you take a case of 250 with you in your car, you may well live to bless the day you made it a habit to do so.

At some shoots there may be one or more walking guns at various drives, who on occasion can enjoy a lot of good sport. A well-filled cartridge-bag slung over the shoulder can prove a tiresome encumbrance in such circumstances. But equally too many cartridges in one's pockets can also be a handicap. I therefore wear a cartridge-belt under my jacket which I have found allows 25 - 30 cartridges to be carried with the weight most comfortably distributed. From this the ten or so kept in my pocket for immediate use in reloading can be replenished as necessary. An advantage in having only a few cartridges in one's pocket at a time is that the brass heads seem to come much more readily to hand, which facilitates quick reloading. But everyone must find out for himself what suits him best in this respect.

There are some well-found rough shoots where there is no transport and it may be advisable to carry a cartridge bag. Obviously one does not want to burden oneself with more weight than necessary. With a hundred-sized bag the number it contains can always be reduced to the appropriate amount. I do not like smaller bags because the opening in the top is also smaller which makes it more difficult for a person with large hands to extract his cartridges easily.

Points for Walking Guns

When walking up your game you may cover considerable distances between shots, and have to give first priority to watching your step. However, in all circumstances it is desirable to be as well prepared for a shot as conditions allow, and to carry your gun with this in

56. The modified ready position

mind. It is awkward and tiring to carry it at the ready position for other than short periods, even where the going permits. But on reasonably level ground a modified ready position can be conveniently adopted with the barrels depressed to an angle of 45° and slanted slightly across the body, as in *Diagram 56*. The stock should be held pressed against the side by the right forearm, which will help to relieve the hands of some of the weight. The left arm should be straight but not rigid, because if it is bent it will pull the muzzles round and up. It will also tend to pull the stock away from the body, and consequently the right hand will tend to go down, which will further elevate the muzzles so that the barrels finish up almost horizontal and pointing straight towards anyone on your left (see *Diagram 57*). If rough going makes it advisable to carry your gun in some other way, say on your shoulder, as per Diagram 45, there are several ways in which you can help yourself to be prepared for a shot. With experience you will develop an eye for country and be able to pick out patches of cover which look the most likely to hold game, so that you can be specially watchful as these are approached. The behaviour of dogs when they are working is always worth studying. Most give clear warning, by their signs of suddenly increased enthusiasm, that a quarry of some kind may shortly be flushed. Some owners even claim that they can tell from their dog's behaviour what the quarry in question will be. But

57. How *Not* to hold your gun when awaiting a shot.
Although the muzzles may start pointing at the ground, the right arm has only to be slightly lowered and they will bear on anyone to the left.

you will need to shoot over a dog on several occasions before you can recognise these finer points, whereas if you are normally observant you should be able to detect the general indication without difficulty, even though some dogs are more demonstrative in this way than others.

When walking up in line, if game is flushed and shot at, the whole line should halt until the person in charge gives the signal to advance again. All guns not directly involved should find a 'platform' for their feet from which they can shoot, and check where it will be safe to do so if required. Even if the quarry concerned has been killed, something may flush, or be flushed, while it is being retrieved. Such pauses are occasions for vigilance rather than relaxation. The commotion of one bird being flushed and shot can instigate the move of others in the same general area, which may wait for a moment before taking flight. So if you immediately seize the opportunity to light a cigarette, you may be caught napping.

Estimating Range
Remarkably few people are good judges of distance. This statement

may be greeted with scepticism, but in my experience it is rare to find anyone, even among those who are country born and bred, who has a natural flair for estimating ranges correctly. It is an accomplishment the majority can only acquire with training and practice. This applies equally to the short distances which concern a sportsman with his gun, as to the longer ones affecting a soldier with a rifle. Every season people tell me they have killed pheasants or other quarry at ranges of 60, 70 and even 100 yds: in some instances where I have been present and so been able to check, the true distances have proved to be between 35 and 45 yds. From the technical viewpoint it is possible to kill a pheasant at 50 yds using a 12-bore with game borings and a standard load of small shot, say No.6's, but beyond this point both pattern-density and pellet-striking energy are failing so fast that to do so can be accounted no more than a fluke. Unhappily some stories of the exploits of famous shots of former times tell of how they killed quarry at exceptional ranges of around 100 yds, and of course we would all like to emulate such feats. Good, modern game-guns used in conjunction with cartridges of similar quality give, if anything, a superior performance to those used by our forbears. So the aspiring shooter, who is realistic, should take such tales with a pinch of salt and accept that for practical purposes his maximum effective range with a game-gun and the standard-load cartridge is 45 yds. If he does so two ranges become of immediate interest — namely 40 yds, at which a quarry is in shot, and 50 yds, at which it is out of shot.

To estimate range it is great help to have a mental picture of something with the length of which you are familiar, so that you can reckon how many times it will fit into the distance you wish to assess. I have found a cricket pitch (i.e. 22 yds) a useful aid in this respect for judging short distances. It has the advantage for the shooting-man that a length of two pitches (44 yds) can be taken for practical purposes as extreme range. For those to whom a cricket pitch is no more than a fragrant memory of their school-days, an alternative is to measure out 20, 40 and 50 yds from a given point on a piece of flat ground, and place a marker at each of these distances. If you then return to your starting point you will gain an idea of what they look like. If you remove in turn the 20-yd and 40-yd markers you will appreciate what comparatively 'long' ranges 40 yds and 50 yds actually appear to be, and might, had you not known, have guessed to be at least 60 and 70 yds respectively.

To get your eye in training for the shooting-season it will repay you to practise estimating ranges when you are out for a walk. This can be done just as well in a town as the country. In a street you can assess the intervals between selected doorways, gate posts, or lamp posts, for example, and then check as you walk along. In the countryside fence-posts, trees, bales of hay and straw and other such objects can be used for the same purpose. In this connection it is useful to know how many paces you take to the 100 yds, and this can easily be checked by walking the length of a football pitch. As a rough guide, a tall man will normally take a stride of a little over 36 in., whereas a short man will have one of rather less — i.e. they will cover 100 yds in about 96 and 104 paces respectively.

Judging ranges in terms of height is a rather trickier problem because the tendency to overestimate is even more pronounced than in the case of those over the level. However it is again a help to have a known yardstick by which to estimate them. The height of a modern two-storey house from ground level to the apex of the roof is around 30 ft. Similarly a so-called tall tree in a wood, shelter-belt or hedgerow is usually in the order of 60 ft high. Trees in really tall stands of beeches or elms may be 100 ft or a little over. The tallest tree I have ever actually been able to measure (because it had been blown down) among a stand of eye-catchingly high beeches, was 110 ft. But trees of such height are exceptional. Taking the example of the 60-ft tree, it is possible to assess at a glance if a bird is only just over tree-top height, half as high again or whatever, or in other words that the vertical range is 20 yds, 30 yds or as the case may be, which is sufficiently accurate for the sportsman's purpose.

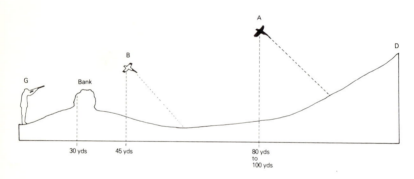

58. A cross-section of ground showing the deceptive effect a false crest can have on estimation of range.
All birds flushing from the dead ground between the Bank and point 'D' where the slope disappears from the shooter's view may seem to him to be rising from just over the Bank, thus misleading him into firing at birds well out of shot as at 'A', especially if they are slipping out to the flank instead of coming forward.

Even experienced judges of distance can be badly deceived by a phenomenon known to Gunners as a 'false crest'. I would never have believed this could be of consequence to sportsmen at the short ranges with which they are concerned, unless I had witnessed a remarkable case in point. A cross-section of the ground in question is shown in *Diagram 58*. As will be seen the drive consisted of a long field of kale sloping gently down to a hedge from which the guns were standing back about 30 yds, in a pasture a few feet below the level of the kale field. This and the fact that the kale field dipped slightly in the approach to the hedge meant that there was about 100 yds of dead ground to the guns in which the approaching beaters were lost to sight. It was into this area that most of the birds ran before they started to flush. As can happen, quite a number of birds, instead of flying straight over the guns, curled away to a flank. The left-hand gun saluted all these with two barrels without touching a feather, because although they appeared to him to be rising only just the other side of the hedge, they were in fact 50 - 70 yds out in the field, and at a range from him of 80 - 100 yds. He was an experienced shot, and completely bewildered by his lack of success until it was explained to him what had happened, and even then he was not entirely convinced that he was not having his leg pulled. Although this is a contingency some shooters may never encounter, it does well illustrate the importance of training the eye to recognise what various quarry look like at different ranges as an aid to judging whether or not they are in shot. It can prove of great advantage when shooting wildfowl over inland waters, and may save you blazing away at duck or geese well out of range, which spoils the sport of others, as well as being a waste of your own cartridges.

The majority of shooters readily concede the importance of being able to judge ranges, yet very few have any idea of how to set about learning to do so. I hope therefore these few ideas may be of help because there is almost no more tiresome companion on a shooting day than one who is continually letting his gun off at birds or ground game which are out of shot.

LOW BIRDS

First Principles

The method of shooting advocated in this book is based on the concept of hitting a moving target with a charge of shot from a gun by relying on the natural powers of coordination of hands and eyes in the same way as these are used to strike a golf or cricket ball. If the technique is properly mastered it will enable you to shoot successfully up to the limits of maximum effective range for game (i.e. 40 - 45 yds), and also using more heavily choked barrels in conjunction with heavier loads of larger shot, to those obtaining for wildfowl (i.e. 50-55 yds). It does not merely suffice for short-range work (say up to 30 yds), and it is not necessary to switch to the swing-and-intercept method for long shots. This latter is based on a different concept, namely that of placing a charge of shot in the air where the target will meet it, or in other words it is equivalent to a cricketer hanging out his bat to intercept the ball instead of making a positive stroke to hit it. Although runs are sometimes scored in this way in the cricket field, it is regarded as a counsel of despair rather than good play; the shooter should look on any 'score' gained from use of the swing-and-intercept method in the same light.

This is simply a summary of what has already been said. But if

117

you are to learn to shoot your best by the method I advocate, it is absolutely vital that you understand it, accept it in principle, and persist in your endeavours to apply it in practice, even when these are not rewarded with the success for which you hoped. When this happens, as it will, you must be prepared to acknowledge to yourself that it is not the method which is at fault but your application of it in some way or other. Timing is of the essence in playing good golf or cricket, and is likewise so in good shooting, where it entails pulling the trigger at precisely the right moment. This applies with particular force to the shooting of low, fast-moving, incoming targets, such as grouse and partridges, where the permissible margin of error is very small, even though you have an effective pattern of approximately 30-in. diameter with which to hit them, as opposed to the slim blade of a cricket bat.

Grouse and Partridges

Both grouse and partridges can be walked up, shot over dogs, (i.e. pointers or setters) or driven. Many sportsmen claim that driven-birds offer by far the most exciting and difficult shooting. From the point of view of the demands made purely on marksmanship this is often true. But those who walk up or shoot over dogs have first to find their quarry and get within range of it, and derive from this element of their sport an interest that is lacking in the shooting of driven-game. To many this more than compensates for the rather lesser demands made on their shooting skill. Although early in the season walked-up or dogged grouse and partridges often offer very simple shots, this has the advantage of allowing you plenty of time to pick your bird and take your shot. It enables the more experienced shooter to select and kill the old birds of a covey, which helps to promote a young and numerous breeding-stock on the ground, and it gives the novice the best chance to put into practice all he has been taught without becoming flustered. In particular he will learn the invaluable lesson that to shoot a bird at too close quarters is simply to 'smash' it, i.e. to put so many shot in it that it is inedible.

Training yourself to select one bird from a covey as your target and then to have eyes for none other until you have completed your shot, plays a major part in success. When a covey is seen as it flushes near at hand, it may appear that you have only to point your gun muzzles in its general direction to be certain of bringing down two, three or more birds. But if you shoot into the 'brown', as this is called, you will probably not touch a feather, because subconsciously your eye will have picked a blank space in the middle, and this is what you will have hit. So however closely bunched a covey may seem, you must always pick one as your target. Where grouse or partridges are lying well you will have plenty of time to do this, and soon acquire the habit. When the coveys rise wilder later in the season, you will have to react more quickly. But it will be when you first take your place in the line to shoot driven-grouse or partridges that you will fully appreciate how time can be of the essence in deciding on your target.

On grouse-moors butts are frequently sited on a reverse slope, allowing you only a very limited field of view to your front. In such a situation a covey can suddenly appear in sight hurtling towards you like a cluster of animated cricket balls. A novice experiencing this for the first time may look wildly from one bird to another, start to mount his gun, change his mind and then, realising the covey is upon him, turn for a shot behind, losing sight of it as he does so. By the time his eyes have picked up the birds again, they will probably be out of range, and he has not fired a shot. Partridges are not as fast flyers as grouse, but still fast enough to cause a similar scene of confusion as they top the hedge in front of the guns unless you are well prepared, and know exactly what you intend to do.

Grouse and partridges in these circumstances are said to need quick shooting. I think this is rather misleading, and would prefer to describe it as decisive shooting, because I believe the secret lies in making a prompt decision on which bird you intend to shoot, and sticking to it. Your intention should be to kill this bird at a range of 40 yds, so as to leave yourself time to shoot another in front with your second barrel. To assist in taking your first shot at this distance, you should have selected some prominent object as a marker — such as a rock or an outstanding clump of heather — at the beginning of the drive, as explained in the previous chapter. But even if you do this, you will probably find that in practice your first bird will actually be hit at nearer 30 yds, so quick is their flight compared with your reaction. Similarly in a partridge-drive when you stand behind a hedge about, or somewhat less than 40 yds to your front, you should try to kill your first bird over the top of the hedge.

To kill two birds of a covey in front in this way is pretty shooting indeed. Even an experienced gun may be well content at the beginning of a day to kill one in front, and then picking his second, to turn with his eyes fastened on it and shoot behind. If you do this, remember as you turn to lower the stock from your shoulder so that the muzzles point up in the air, and not at your neighbouring gun (see *Diagram 55*).

When a covey is coming straight towards you the question arises which bird should you choose as your target. If no special safety factor affects the issue, I suggest it ought to be the first one that catches your eye. If you dither around trying to evaluate which will give you the easiest shot, you will miss your opportunity altogether.

It is a wonderful feeling when it suddenly dawns on you that you have a right and left within your grasp. But to achieve this you have to kill the first bird with your first barrel, and to do this you must keep your eyes fixed relentlessly on it until you have pulled the trigger and seen it crumple in the air. All too many right and lefts fail to come to fruition because the shooter switches his eyes away in search of the second target before he has finished dealing with the first. To make a single barrel kill, you must concentrate on one target only. If you succeed with your first barrel, it is quite time enough then to seek to crown this achievement with your second. Some years ago I was able to watch a very fine shot in action at a grouse drive, because owing to the strength and direction of the wind no birds came my way, and as I was in the flank butt higher up the hill I had a grandstand view. The point of interest was not how many difficult birds he killed, but how few easy ones he missed. I believe this was because he took just as much trouble over the latter as the former. It seems to me that if we all appreciated that it is just as easy to miss a simple bird as it is hard to hit a difficult one, we might all shoot a little better.

As regards putting our drill into effect for these low birds, you should assume the ready position at the same time as you select your target, with your feet placed as in *Diagram 34* and weight rather on the front foot. Some people advocate advancing the left foot slightly to help you lean into your shot, but this should not be necessary, and may handicap you in turning quickly to use your second barrel. When you see the moment has come to take your shot, bring the gun to your shoulder in one incisive movement, as already described, and at the instant your eyes tell you the muzzles are on target pull the trigger. You must remain 'stiff necked' throughout, and if you have synchronised your actions correctly you should kill every time. The overthrow required for these incoming birds at little more than head-height is extremely small even when they are travelling at their fastest. Though it may sound surprising, due to the impression of speed they give, they are easily missed in front because the shooter delays momentarily in pulling the trigger. When we miss we automatically assume it has been behind, so to correct matters in this sort of situation we delay even longer in pulling the trigger next time, and in consequence miss still further in front. So if you suffer a series of seemingly inexplicable misses at driven-grouse or partridges, try shooting the pants off the next one; I have found it virtually a sovereign remedy in such circumstances. It should certainly bring home the importance of trusting your eye implicitly. If you do this, and your timing is right, such targets will be no problem. Do not confuse 'timing', by which I mean pulling the trigger at exactly the right moment, with 'accuracy'. If your gun fits you, you mount it correctly, and your timing is right, you *will* be accurate and need have no worries on this score. If you start thinking in terms of 'accuracy', it will merely incite you to begin taking conscious aim, and that, as should be clear by now, is fatal to good shooting. So forget the word, it has no relevance in this context.

You may be told on occasion when shooting both grouse and partridges to keep well down in your butt, because if the birds see you they will turn away to a flank instead of coming forward properly. If, once you have disposed of the preliminaries outlined in the previous Chapter, you can develop the art of sitting or standing still you will minimise the risk of your presence alarming and deflecting approaching coveys. You should also eschew unnecessary chatter.

120

Human movement and noise are the two things that most surely catch the attention of wild creatures and cause them to take avoiding action. A covey feeding a short distance in front of the butts may on becoming alarmed simply crouch where it is, and not take flight until it sees others of its kind on the move. If it then decides to slip out to a flank or fly back over the beaters, it may give a lead which others follow, and so ruin the beat. A person who chatters away and keeps continually bobbing up and down like a jack-in-the-box in his butt can easily be the cause of such a debâcle. A hatless head, especially if it is partially bald, shows up vividly at a distance as something out of harmony with the rest of the landscape, so it is advisable to wear a quiet-coloured hat or cap.

Although I have considered the shooting of grouse and partridges together because they often offer much the same type of target, and so to that extent require similar treatment by the shooter, the pace and flight of the one are very different from those of the other, as are the characteristics of the countryside in which each are normally shot. So just as a cricketer starts his innings by playing himself in to accustom his eyes to the vagaries of the bowling and pitch, so a shooter needs to do the same when tackling different quarry in different surroundings. In particular a person accustomed to shooting over enclosed land may find his eyes take a little while to adjust to the wide open spaces of a grouse-moor before he can judge distances with equal facility. Also a shooter must be just as alive to what a change in the 'bowling' may portend as a cricketer. Thus if, when you are shooting grouse, a blackcock appears, you should immediately say to yourself that although its flight appears less hurried it is in fact a faster flying bird, and pause momentarily for a good look at it to allow your eyes to register the difference before you take your shot. If you do this a blackcock should prove no more difficult to kill cleanly than a grouse. The basic reason for many being missed each season is failure to take this simple precaution. The rough-shooter, who is never quite certain what quarry he will next encounter, is accustomed to dealing with each shot on its merits. But the driven-game shooter, who enjoys a lot of sport at one particular quarry, will naturally develop a set rhythm in his shooting, and must remember the need to adapt this when the quarry changes.

Walked-up Pheasants
Walked-up pheasants generally offer low shots within the meaning of the term, though sometimes they can quickly attain a surprising height and speed, especially in hilly country with a stiff breeze blowing, which puts them on a par with a good driven-bird. When walked up in kale or roots in October they often lie very close, and flush only a few yards in front of you, climb to no great height, and fly straight away from you. They look a very easy target. Yet quite frequently they are handsomely missed with both barrels, and not only by inexperienced shots. There are usually two reasons for this.

121

Firstly, the commotion the bird makes when flushed flusters the shooter, whose instinctive reaction is to shoot quickly before it escapes out of range, and as a result he shoots too soon. Secondly, on a dry day a well-plumaged pheasant generally departs in a steep climb, so that the over-eager gun fires his first barrel under it. But having gained a height of about 15 ft or so it then flattens out, and wings away as fast as it can, causing a miss behind with the second barrel, because the shooter has failed to take this change into account.

The correct way to take this shot is to pause when the bird flushes, and position your feet properly. Simultaneously bring your gun to the ready position, fixing your eyes on the bird as you do so. It will probably follow a course similar to that depicted in *Diagram 59* — i.e. a rapid ascent followed by level flight. When your target is nearing 30 yds, mount your gun to the shoulder and shoot, so that you kill at this range, point **C** in the diagram. This will leave you ample time for a face-saving second barrel before it is out of range, if you have muffed the first. A common reason for missing this type of shot is bobbing the head down to meet the stock instead of bringing the latter right up to the cheek. Making the brief pause mentioned above, and so taking just that little bit of extra time and trouble over your shot, will help you to avoid this fault.

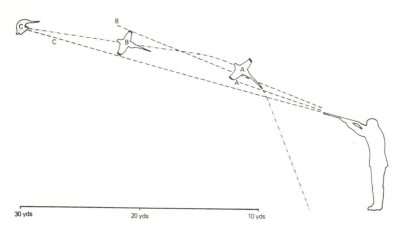

30 yds   20 yds   10 yds

59. How to shoot a walked-up pheasant.
Many walked-up pheasants are missed because the shooter fires too soon, missing under with his first barrel, as at 'A', and behind with his second, as at 'B'. The correct way to take such birds is to allow them to level out in flight and shoot them at about 30 yds, as at 'C'.

This is the classic shot at walked-up pheasants, with which many a newcomer is confronted the first time he takes the field in their pursuit. There will be many variations that you will encounter, in some of which the length of the target will be of consequence (e.g. a

122

crossing bird), and to deal successfully with these you must fix your eyes on the head, as explained in Chapter 4.

Snipe

Walked-up snipe can provide some of the finest sport you are ever likely to enjoy, and some of the trickiest targets. There is a lot of folklore concerning how best you can come to terms with them, which old stagers at the game will recount with relish and rub their hands with glee, albeit in the nicest possible way, when any lack of success on your part can be attributed to failure to observe such excellent precepts. But don't be put off. Snipe-shooting is certainly something of a specialised art, but with practice any reasonably competent marksman can master it.

The purpose of this book is to try to tell you how to shoot, not how to organise shooting, except as this may be relevant to the former. I do not therefore propose to fuel the flames of controversy by placing on record my own views of how snipe bogs may best be walked. My impression is that, with rare exceptions, a host at a snipe-shoot is looking forward to enjoying a day watching you miss, and to savour this to the full will ensure that you get plenty of opportunities for doing so.

When walking a bog, with water possibly over your knees, you must be prepared to dispense with the benefits of footwork. You need to keep your eyes on the general area of the ground about 20 yds to your front. The first indication you have of a snipe jumping may be the sound of the soft screech it gives as it does so, followed by a sight of the flash of its white rump as it zig-zags away. Stop and obtain as well-balanced a footing as you can. Then fix your eyes really intently on it, and take your shot.

Some people say you should shoot as soon as a snipe jumps, before it starts to zig-zag, others that you should wait until it has straightened out in flight. In my experience it is best merely to concentrate on getting on to the bird as quickly as you can. Your eye will soon become familiar with their erratic flight, and able to judge the critical moment to shoot. Indecision is fatal; in this, probably more than in any other type of shooting, you must devote your whole concentration to the target, and when your eyes say 'fire', mount your gun and pull the trigger in one spontaneous, briskly executed movement. If you dither with the butt at the shoulder, and start to waggle the muzzles around trying to improve on your first aim, you will be lost.

Avoid shooting at excessive range. A snipe rising at 30 yds should be killable within 40 yds, even if you have a first-barrel miss. It is a small target, and a high pattern-density is therefore needed to ensure a clean kill. A 12-bore with game borings and a standard load of No.8 shot will provide the requisite pattern-density up to 35 - 40 yds. So a snipe killed at 30 yds or over can be considered a genuinely long shot. If snipe are rising wild, nothing is more exasperating than a companion who keeps shooting at, and missing, birds at extreme range, as this disturbs those that might lie close enough to offer a fair shot, and there are always a minority that will do so given the chance.

Driven-snipe may come to the guns scudding low over the ground, or as high as a tolerably well shown driven-pheasant. If you treat the former like an incoming grouse, they should pose no special problem. But the latter sometimes appear almost to twinkle and to be quite slow moving; in consequence a shooter is inclined to dwell on his aim, instead of snapping the gun to his shoulder and pulling the trigger. So once again, take a good look at your target, and then trust your eyes to call the shot correctly for you.

In conclusion, snipe-shooting makes no less a demand on physical fitness than marksmanship, and you must also acquire the knack of 'bog trotting', i.e. the ability to walk a bog without undue mishaps or noise. Only if you are equally sound in all these three respects can you hope to become a really successful snipe-shot.

Miscellaneous

There are two further birds that deserve a special mention, as each may pose problems for the shooter peculiar to their species. The Golden Plover can offer splendid sport, especially in a strong wind. They are mainly to be found in Scotland, the North of England, North Wales, some Devonshire moors, and parts of Ireland. On their feeding-grounds in winter they sometimes gather in flocks of several hundred, though smaller flocks of a dozen or 20 are quite common. On windless days they are not worth pursuing, because when disturbed they simply rise in the air, and mill around right out of shot. But with a really strong wind blowing they will keep low, and if you can then conceal yourself on their flight-line, you should be able to enjoy some rare sport.

They are reckoned to be one of our fastest flying sporting birds, and from my experience well deserve this reputation. They dip and swerve in their flight, and a flock coming towards you gives the impression of an approaching wave. When you fire your first barrel the whole flock will almost invariably swoop down, seemingly straight at you, which to the unitiated can be slightly unnerving. So this is another species at which you should take a good look so that your eyes can register the idiosyncracies of their flight. Start by being content to shoot one bird out of each flock that comes over you. When you have succeeded in doing this two or three times consecutively with your first barrel, then you will be on the way to becoming master of the situation, and can begin trying for rights and lefts.

Making yourself pick one of a closely-bunched covey of partridges as your target is often difficult enough, but compared to selecting one of an approaching flock of 'goldies' it is child's play. Nevertheless you must do so, or you will never get on terms with them. To make it as easy as possible for yourself, pick the bird you intend as your target just before you are going to shoot, then mount your gun and pull the trigger as soon as the muzzles are on target. If you trust your eyes, your hands will respond by providing all the impulsion necessary to induce the overthrow you need. Once you have got the timing right, there are only two things you need concentrate on; first, bringing your gun correctly to the shoulder, and second, remaining stiff-necked as you do so. If you observe this simple routine, you should soon find you are knocking 'goldies' out of the sky with the same facility as you have killed grouse or partridges.

The ubiquitous woodpigeon can offer a greater variety of shots than almost any other quarry. But the one I have found of particular interest within the context of this chapter is the bird you may encounter when shooting over decoys, which on a rather windless day comes swooping down to join the party. Your unashamedly professional pigeon shooter may tell you that you are mad not to let him land, and then to shoot him on the ground. If you regard shooting these birds purely as a pest-control operation, there is nothing more to be said. However if you treat their shooting as also a sporting occasion, taking advantage of those that have settled in trees or on the ground will be an exception to the rule.

On a fairly still day woodpigeon can drop like stones into your decoys from a considerable height, and their rate of descent is very rapid indeed. Unless you properly appreciate this, you will shoot well over the top of them. The ideal time to take these birds is just as they spread their wings prior to landing, when if you concentrate on shooting their legs off, you should kill every time. You can quickly get the measure of them in this way, but I find after a time it becomes rather tedious, and enjoy the greater challenge of trying to take them earlier in their approach. But if woodpigeon are coming freely to your decoys one of the advantages is that you have considerable latitude in how difficult or easy you like to make each shot for yourself.

When decoying with a strong wind at your back, the birds will make their descent some way out, and then approach up wind to the decoys. In these circumstances you should treat them like driven-grouse or partridges, paying due regard to their rather different flight, although for practical shooting purposes this is not of great significance.

You may hear people talking at length about pigeon 'taking a lot of shot', and so forth. In fact a woodpigeon is not a terribly fast flyer. But it does have keen sight, quick reactions, and a marked capacity for aerial manoevre, which enable it to take last-minute evading action and so escape your pattern altogether, or at least the bulk of it. However a woodpigeon properly centred in a shotgun-pattern is just as vulnerable as any other quarry. To prove this for yourself, you should sit absolutely still in your hide until you are ready to take your shot, then snap the gun to your shoulder and pull the trigger in a quick, decisive movement, as opposed to a rushed one.

In my experience a 1-oz. load of No.7 shot is the most lethal for woodpigeon, because it is pattern-density rather than pellet-striking energy that is needed to ensure a clean kill.

Any winged quarry can of course on occasion present the shooter with a low-flying target. But I have tried in this chapter to deal with those most likely to do so, the circumstances which commonly prevail, and how these may affect your shooting. With certain notable exceptions, a low bird is mentally classified by most sportsmen as an easy shot. I believe this is often the reason for it being missed, because the shooter does not bother to concentrate properly on his target, or on mounting his gun correctly to the shoulder. You can avoid this pitfall if you train yourself to stigmatise no shot as easy until the bird is dead in the air. Finally, remember any shot at a low-flying target is a potentially dangerous one, unless you have a clear field of fire; always make sure you do before you pull the trigger.

HIGH BIRDS

Height and its Implications for the Shooter
The shooting of high birds is associated in the minds of most sportsmen with pheasants, but some species of wildfowl may be even faster on the wing and offer equally high shots, and so make no less exacting demands on your marksmanship. More exceptionally certain other quarry may come high, fast, and handsomely to the guns. But first let us be clear what constitute truly high birds, and the degree to which these ought to be sub-classified.

Let us start by choosing a realistic datum line to distinguish the highest low birds from the lowest high ones. It was explained in Chapter 11 that a reasonably modern two-storey house is about 30 ft tall. A pheasant at that height would be considered low though shootable, whereas a partridge would be thought quite high. At 40 ft a pheasant would be described as fairly well up, while a partridge would rate as a definitely high bird. I think therefore if we select 40 ft as our arbitrary dividing-line, it will be about right.

Many pheasants crossing the guns at 60 - 70 ft are said to be high, but are really only of middling height compared with their counter-parts flushed from the tops of the Sussex/Dorset Downs or a Scottish/Welsh hillside, which fly at 90 ft or more. So I suggest our so-called high birds can be realistically graded in three categories, namely, those between 40 and 60 ft which we can call 'well up', those at 60 - 90 ft which are 'middling high', and those at 90 - 120 ft which are genuinely 'high'. For future reference let us assume these terms have the meanings thus ascribed to them.

Diagram 60 shows the effect target-height has on range over the ground. The 40-yd arc, **T1 - T2**, makes it plain that the higher the bird the closer you must let it come in, so that it is properly within shooting distance. But it is interesting to note that it isn't until a bird is flying at over 40 ft that the range, gun to target, begins to differ materially from that over the ground. Thus a bird at point **D** in the

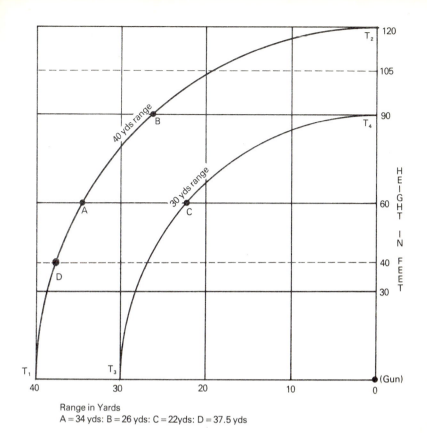

Range in Yards
A = 34 yds: B = 26 yds: C = 22yds: D = 37.5 yds

60. The effect of target-height on range over the ground.

diagram is a mere $2\frac{1}{2}$ yds inside the 40 yd mark on the ground, which for practical shooting-purposes is insignificant. However, a comparable bird flying at 60 ft (point **A** on the diagram), is six yds inside the same mark on the ground, which is significant, and the difference becomes markedly more so as the altitude of the bird increases from thereon. A 30-yd shot is a reasonably long one, and many shooters would prefer to shoot their bird at this range rather than 40 yds if circumstances allowed, so a 30-yd arc, **T3** - **T4**, has been included for comparative purposes. The point I hope the diagram makes amply clear is the need to allow 'high' birds, as defined above, to come right in so that you shoot them only 10 - 20 yds in front as measured over the ground, though the actual range, gun to target, is between 30 and 40 yds. If you allow middling high birds to come similarly well in, you will be shooting them at 25 - 30 yds, which is a fair distance. I have heard it said that driven-pheasants should be taken as far out as possible. I consider this bad

127

advice, because it can lead to shooting at excessive range, and encourages a shooter to make a shot as difficult, instead of as easy as possible for himself, thereby increasing the likelihood of wounding instead of killing cleanly. Also, unlike grouse and partridges, pheasants do not normally come forward in such close formation or numbers as to make this necessary. So allow a pheasant, or any other quarry that is flying 'well up' or higher, to come well in before you shoot: you will make it an easier, more killable target for yourself. There can be no objection to this on grounds of poor sportsmanship, as people sometimes fear. But I would emphasise that low pheasants (i.e. those below 40 ft) are a different matter, and if they come straight to you at a drive are best left alone; always remember you have been invited to a sporting occasion, not a massacre.

High birds are said to call for 'accurate' shooting. As explained in Chapter 4, you must not think of this in terms of aiming, as with a rifle. Assuming you have a well fitting gun, and the actions of your hands are properly coordinated with the dictates of your eyes, your accuracy will depend solely on the precision of your gun-mounting. *Diagram 61* shows the effects of errors in gun-mounting on the placing of the 30-in. pattern at the ranges indicated. If the muzzles are approximately 1 in. out of correct alignment at **G** due to faulty gun-mounting, the charge will be centred at **T2** instead of **T1**, which will entail a clean miss. At 40 yds range, the equivalent error at the muzzles would need to be only a little over $\frac{3}{4}$ in. to produce the same result. So if we have a high bird down, merely hard hit instead of well killed, it will mean we have made the maximum permissible error in muzzle-alignment of around only $\frac{1}{4}$ in. If our target is at **T3** - **T4** the consequences of any error are aggravated, because as the target is not at right angles to the line of fire the pattern is slightly elongated, and therefore thinner. I hope this makes clear how little the spread of the pattern compensates for the errors of 'aim', or more correctly gun-mounting, when you are shooting high birds. Your gun-mounting must therefore be as near perfect as you can make it in order to deal successfully with such quarry. But if your gun really fits you, and you take the trouble to give yourself the necessary practice, there is no reason at all why you should not readily gain the requisite mastery, just as does a good golfer in the handling of his clubs.

Shooting High Birds
Some sportsmen, including many who should know better, get in a terrible flap when they have to deal with really high pheasants. They equip themselves with guns with heavily choked barrels and cartridges with larger loads of bigger shot. If you do this, or because such heavy artillery is not available to you harbour doubts about the capacity of your game-gun with a standard-load cartridge to deliver the goods, you have in effect admitted defeat at the hands of the birds before a shot has been fired.

If you wish to achieve comparable success with high birds to that

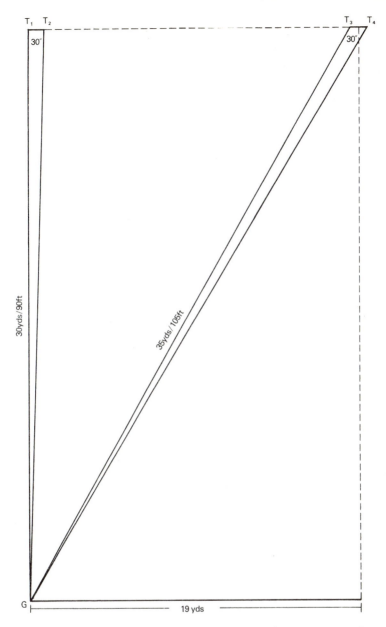

61. The effect of errors in gun-mounting on centring the pattern correctly.

which you know you can attain with others, you must start confident in the knowledge that it is within your capacity to do so. In soldierly parlance, you must be imbued with the will to win. To gain this happy frame of mind, you must be absolutely convinced on two points: the first is that a properly-centred pattern of a standard load of No.6 shot fired from an improved-cylinder 12-bore barrel will kill a 120-ft-high pheasant stone dead; the second is that to shoot such a pattern calls for no exceptional 'magic', but only the efficient application of the 'magic' you have already been taught. As regards pattern; from the information in Chapter 2 (Tables 4 and 11), we can expect a pattern-density in the 30-in. circle of 144, against a requirement of 100 (Table 6), and an individual pellet striking-energy of 1.43 ft lb. (Table 8) against a requirement of 1.00 ft/lb. (Table 7). Our needs in both these respects are therefore more than adequately met. Turning now to execution, let us see what special calls are made on our skill, and how these can also be met.

In many places where high birds are presented to the guns they may come into view 300 - 400 yds away, and so take about a quarter of a minute to arrive within shot. When you are keyed up this can seem a very long time indeed, and the urge to get on with the shooting becomes more and more compelling as the seconds tick away. However, as has already been explained, to start mounting your gun prematurely will only engender failure, so you must control your natural impatience. There is no point in even adopting the ready position too soon, because if you do you will become over-tensed, which is likely to impair the spontaneity of your subsequent actions. You will soon learn from experience how much time you have in hand. When you take these high shots you must allow your weight to flow back smoothly on to the right foot with the left heel lifting as this happens (see *Diagram 36*.) So when you see your target approaching, first make sure your feet are correctly positioned. Then in due course you can bring your gun to the ready position; I suggest when the bird is about 100 yds away, measured at ground level. You should then fix your eyes firmly on its *head*, and allow your hands to bring the muzzles to bear so that you have in golfing parlance 'addressed the bird'. From now on, until you have completed your shot, you must remain stiff-necked. Your eyes will begin to assess the pace of the target, which you will probably realise is much faster than you had originally thought.

I wrote in Chapter 4 that when you take your shot you must make a positive movement or 'stroke' with the gun, just as you do with your bat when you are hitting a cricket ball. This is vitally important if you are to shoot high birds successfully. If it helps you to accomplish this, imagine you are going to hit the incoming bird to the boundary with the muzzles. If you do this, keep your eyes on it, and shoot at it, i.e. pull the trigger when the muzzles pass its head — you will be surprised how readily these high birds come tumbling out of the sky.

Some people, in my view totally mistakenly, may tell you that all you have to do is point your gun correctly and fire, which is snap-shooting by any other name. This is a catastrophic over-simplification because it leads people to believe that no gun-movement is involved. How wrong this is, is quite clearly shown in

Diagram 51, where the gun-muzzles have moved through an arc, from 'a' to 'd', of approximately 40°, 'a' being the point at which the trigger was pulled. The distance 'a' - 'd' is equivalent to the follow-through of the bat in cricket after the ball has been hit. But in shooting, because the target is in a line in direct extension of the muzzles (as the trigger is pulled), it is struck at 'b' during the follow-through or 'overthrow', as we call it. Most of us play cricket, hockey, tennis, squash, or some such game before we start to shoot with a shotgun. If we make a stroke to help the ball on its way, we know we have to do so with the bat/stick/racquet accelerating through the line of the ball. If we wish to shoot incoming birds or crossing birds/ground game, we must handle our gun in precisely the same way.

So if you will trust your eyes and allow your hands to react instinctively according to their dictates, I suggest the requirements for shooting high birds proficiently can be summarised as follows:

(a) Make sure you have a correct, comfortable stance on firm ground.

(b) Don't assume the ready position too soon.

(c) When you do come to the ready position, fix your eyes on the *head* of the quarry.

(d) When your eyes tell you the moment has come to take your shot, move your gun up into the shoulder as if you were going to hit the bird a full-blooded blow with the muzzles, pulling the trigger just as they pass its head, and the butt has bedded home at the shoulder.

But remember that, in the final analysis, everything depends on you mounting your gun correctly, so spare no effort to make sure this is so well rehearsed that it is intuitive. If you make this so, and follow the drill given above, then dealing with high birds of any kind, even wild geese, should pose no problem that you cannot master. One final point; it is absolutely crucial when shooting high birds that you look at the head, and not just 'at them'. The jingle below may help you to do this:

How many would succeed, who fail,
If pheasants hadn't so much tail.

At a shoot where the pheasants come really well to the guns, it is sometimes very noticeable that the number of hens killed far exceeds that of the cocks, although there was no such disparity in numbers facing the guns. Keepers and others are inclined to attribute this to the faster flight of the cocks, but if you watch birds of both sexes, flushed from the same area, going forward, you will see that this is by no means always true. I believe in fact it is due to the cock's longer tail causing those who only look at the bird, instead of at its head, to miss behind. This is further substantiated by the temporary loss of form many good marksmen used to experience when they first came to shoot driven-pheasants, after dealing successfully for several weeks with driven partridges, where merely looking at the bird sufficed.

With wild duck and geese the problem is slightly different, because instead of having a long tail trailing behind them, they have a long neck sticking out in front, and therefore where a cock pheasant would simply get its tail-feathers tickled by the pellets on the fringe of the pattern, the unfortunate duck or goose is struck in the stern. So when shooting these birds it is if anything even more important to observe the principle of looking at the head, because in essence your pattern will be centred where you look.

GROUND GAME

Some Relevant Factors

For the purpose of this book the term 'ground game' embraces hares and rabbits only. But the principles involved in their shooting apply equally to other small quadrupeds, subject to due allowance being made for difference in movement and so on of the latter.

Although rabbits are classified at law as pests, whereas hares rate as game, and rabbits more rarely scream when wounded in the piteous manner of hares, I hate to see botched shots at the former just as much as the latter. In former times some sportsmen considered any old cartridges were good enough for shooting rabbits, and used to buy cheap imported brands for this purpose. These often gave rather sub-standard ballistics, so that at even moderate ranges the pellets lacked adequate penetration, with the result that animals were sometimes hit and wounded when they should have been killed. This is both unsatisfactory and inhumane. So although rabbit populations have increased again in some places to the extent that a quite surprising number of cartridges can be fired by two or three guns in the course of an evening's sport, for the sake of your quarry and your own self-respect as a marksman avoid trying to save a few pennies by buying cheap cartridges. They are likely to prove a bad investment.

A rabbit started from a tuft of grass in a field can appear to move like the proverbial greased lightning. It certainly makes a very quick getaway, probably faster than that of a hare, but it is doubtful if a rabbit at full stretch ever exceeds 30 m.p.h., whereas a hare has been paced at almost 40 m.p.h. This means that even at their best speeds they are substantially slower moving than in normal circumstances are the winged quarry we shoot. It is important to recognise this because otherwise the impression of speed given by ground game can upset your timing, in that it causes you to bring the gun smartly to the shoulder, realise you have got there too soon and pause in pulling the trigger, so that as a result you miss behind.

A hare is a large animal with an average weight of 7 - 8 lb. Some giants of over 13 lb have been killed in England. Although these were recorded in the last century, it seems not unreasonable to suppose beasts of a more modest 10 lb., say, may be encountered to-day. One effect of a hare's size is that people are apt to take shots at excessive range, especially when shooting over open plough or downland where it is difficult to make an accurate snap-judgement of distance. I have found a useful rule-of-thumb as to whether or not a hare is in range is if you can look it in the eye. People with reasonably good normal eyesight should be able to do this up to about 35 yds. If you train yourself to do it, it will help you not only to avoid taking out-of-range shots, but also to centre your pattern correctly and avert the embarassment of a cripple limping away, trailing a hindleg.

Stationary Targets
Although this heading may seem to flout the finest traditions of British sportsmanship, there may be times when you wish or have to deal with a sitting hare or rabbit, or indeed some other creature. Unless you want to provide the beaters with a topic for hilarity to enjoy over their beer in the local hostelry at the end of the day, it is a shot you will wish to be able to execute efficiently in one go.

In Chapter 2 I mentioned that a properly regulated sporting-gun centres its pattern 4 in. high at 40 yds. With any sort of rising bird you will have learnt instinctively to hold the muzzles 'well up' on the target. Unless you make due allowance for these two factors in dealing with stationary quarry on the ground, they will cause you to shoot over the top of your target. You should therefore aim to shoot the ground from under such targets, see *Diagram 62*. You will find the same applies in principle when taking a direct crossing-shot at ground game on level terrain, and even more so when it is a downhill one, as depicted in *Diagram 63*.

Shooting Hares
A hare is a much more prized addition to the bag on the Continent than in Britain, where a sportsman's view is well summed up by the old adage, 'He who shoots a hare, carries it!'. It is not surprising therefore that on the whole our continental cousins are much better hare shots than we are. Yet a hare on open ground, over which most are shot in this country, offers a basically very simple and killable target, if the shooter performs his 'drill' properly in taking the shot. There is one exception, and that is a hare going straight away at 30 yds or more, when its rump obtrudes so massively in the line of fire that even though you shoot well up between its ears, it is very difficult to ensure it is hit well forward and killed cleanly. I prefer to forgo such opportunities, though at closer quarters a straight going-away hare can be bowled over as easily as a rabbit.

I believe there are two matters at the heart of the hare-shooting problem. Many sportsmen do not like to risk merely wounding a hare, and so would rather not shoot at one at all. Thus when they think they are obliged to do so, they make only a half-hearted attempt, and are in consequence certain to muff their shot before they

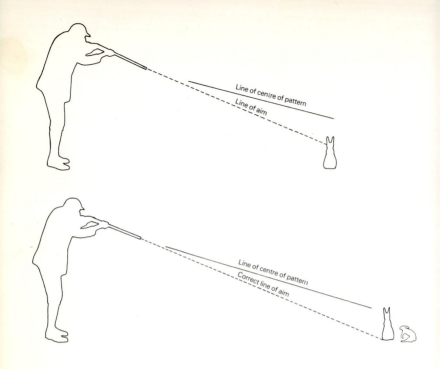

62. How to shoot a stationary target.
With a stationary target, such as a feeding rabbit may present, you must 'aim' to shoot the ground from under it.

have even raised their gun. Secondly, few people either take a good enough look at their target, or realise they must look at it in the right place, namely the head. As a result they find their timing is all awry, as already explained above, or their pattern is incorrectly centred, and the hare is hit behind instead of forward.

The only way the reluctant hare-shot will ever overcome his reluctance is by gaining self-confidence, and he will only achieve this if he knows what to do, and is able to practise doing it. It has long surprised me that no shooting-school in Britain has to my knowledge a 'falling plate type' electric hare. The I.M.I. 'running rabbit type' clay is an entirely inadequate substitute, because although you can learn to break it with great facility, it presents the wrong picture to the eye one from which you cannot learn to avoid hitting a hare up the backside.

Shooting Rabbits
A rabbit has much less length than a hare, but a well-grown wild specimen may measure 15 in. from the tip of its nose to the end of its rump. So looking at its head is still an important factor in successful shooting. Dealing with rabbits in the open should pose no special

134

problem if you perform your "drill" correctly. In particular, if a rabbit flushes close at hand when you are walking up, don't let its apparent speed cause you to rush your shot. If you have a clear field of fire treat it in this respect like your walked-up pheasant, and aim to bowl it over at about 30 yds. If, however, you cannot give it any liberty because it is bolting for nearby cover, you will simply have to make the best shot you can. With a straight going-away shot you should look well up between its ears in order to ensure you hit it well forward and kill it cleanly.

Shooting rabbits in cover is a very different proposition. They can offer a most elusive target as they bounce along, disappearing intermittently behind hazel stools, patches of brambles and other low cover. But you must not be put off by this. Fix your eyes on their head. Once you have assessed the quarry's line and pace, make up your mind where you are going to take your shot. Then do so, ignoring any cover behind which it may temporarily vanish on the way there. If you follow this procedure you should be bowling them over in great style, with only the occasional hazel stool becoming the unintended victim.

Special Considerations
Nearly all countrymen have one thing in common, they enjoy a bit of sport with rabbits, irrespective of whether it is being a member of a ferreting expedition, one of a party of guns with their dogs walking up rabbits in rough cover, or participating in a formal day's shooting, where rabbits merely feature among the 'various'. In fact one rabbit well killed by a walking-gun may earn him more acclaim from the beaters than any number of pheasants as expertly dispatched. This sort of special undercurrent of excitement that rabbit-shooting of any kind generates can make it very tempting to risk a

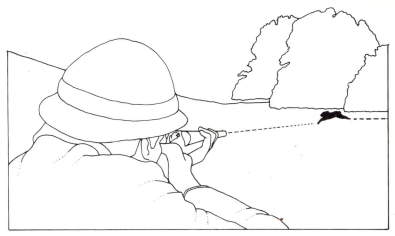

63. How to take a downhill crossing-shot at ground game.
Treat this kind of shot in the same way as a stationary target, or you will shoot over it.

rash shot. You must never allow yourself to succumb, and if you are in charge of the day's sport, never be too diffident to make it quite clear to your fellow guns at the meet in a suitably tactful manner that this is the way things are to be. In particular:

(a) If you are ferreting, everyone must remain in position until you give the word that operations at the bury in question are finished, when the guns will unload, and there will be no further shooting on the site. When guns are placed in position they should be given definite arcs of fire to which they must restrict their shooting, and be warned to allow rabbits to bolt well clear of the bury before they shoot.

(b) If you are walking-up rabbits in cover of any kind, everyone must stay in line, and this applies equally to beaters. If it is necessary for someone to drop back to pick up a rabbit, the line must stop until he rejoins it. Avoid having too widely spread a line; about five yards between individuals is sufficient. Owing to people having to go round clumps of cover, the line is bound to become disorganised from time to time, so pause whenever necessary to allow for readjustment. If dogs are working, rabbits must be allowed to get reasonably clear of cover before they are shot, or a dog will sooner or later become a casualty as well.

When shooting rabbits in cover, you must be fully alive to the danger of ricochets off stones, tree-stumps, etc., and ensure you observe the maxim, 'Never shoot, where you cannot see'.

At hare-shoots, where there may be 30, or 40 or more guns, some of whom walk with the beaters while the remainder stand, the safety-problem is rather different. Such shoots require first-class organisation and firm control by the person in charge. The standing guns will conceal themselves as best they may. As the beat approaches an agreed signal should be given, usually a blast on a whistle or horn, after which there is to be no shooting to their front by either standing or walking guns. A hare, especially when approaching the line of beaters, will often jink first one way and then the other as it makes up its mind which gap to make a dash for, and sometimes change its mind at the last moment. Gaps between individuals in the line may be 15 - 20 yds or more. If you have stopped to prepare for a shot, found the hare has turned away, but just as you start to walk forward again discover it has altered course once more and is returning, you may have inadvertently got well out of line. If you now take your shot without further ado, you can find you have done so dangerously close to someone else.

Where a line of 40 - 50 beaters and guns is sweeping across undulating, though open land, it is almost impossible for one man to exercise close control. I therefore always like to see a number of keepers dispersed at intervals along the line on these occasions, so that they can assist in keeping necessary control. However, even when this is done, it still remains the responsibility of each gun to make sure he does not swing through, or shoot too close to anyone

136

else in the line, because the danger of ricocheting pellets, even on apparently soft ground such as plough, should never be underrated.

In some places hare-drives are an annual event, and necessary to control numbers. If properly organised, with a team of safe, competent guns in attendance, not only do they well serve their purpose, but also provide good sport. Unfortunately this is by no means always the case, and arrangements often leave much to be desired. As a result a shooting-man often rather thankfully declines an invitation to a hare-drive, which on the Continent would be welcomed. If only they were better organised, the sporting value of the quarry might be more fully appreciated.

8 the man most likely to miss —and why

General

The aim of this book has been, and still is, to tell you how to hit moving quarry with a charge of shot from a game gun. However, we are human and fallible, and consequently from time to time we all miss, even the best of shots. When we do, we should know where, and if we think about it, be able to make a good guess at why.

This Chapter is headed 'The Man Most Likely to . . .'. This may seem slightly at odds with modern anti-discriminatory legislation. But the Bible states that Christmas is a time of goodwill towards men, and makes no mention of women, so I hope I follow sound precedent, and that every shooting person, irrespective of their sex, will understand that that means 'YOU', because women miss too, and nothing can make them more equal than that!

Why You Miss

The late Robert Churchill maintained that the majority of misses were attributable to head movement in the interval between 'addressing' the target and pulling the trigger. I would not disagree with this, but in my experience there are other quite common causes as well, such as premature gun mounting. But before dealing with such points, it is worth considering three more fundamental factors, which if not always the actual cause of a miss, may have contributed largely to it. They are:-

1. Lack of knowledge of how to 'play' the shot
2. Lack of practice
3. Lack of shooting fitness.

How Knowledge Helps

The art of game shooting was long regarded as an inexplicable mystery which only a minority of naturally gifted people could master, and the majority, not so blessed, couldn't. Unfortunately this myth has become so enshrined in shooting lore, that it is still blindly accepted by many shooting men to-day. It is the principal reason why so large a number remain poor or indifferent shots to the end of their days; they are convinced that they can do little or nothing materially to improve their performance, and therefore it is a waste of money to try. This is absolute nonsense.

It is accepted without question that playing golf is basically a matter of coordination of hands and eyes; game shooting is the same. The aspiring shot must start out by understanding this, and being utterly convinced of it. It is the fundamental concept of the method of shooting I have tried to explain in this book.

The technique of game shooting, like that of golf, is not easy to master, and both dedication and determination are needed in order to do so. A golfer will study the lie of his ball, also the distance to the green, and then make up his mind how to play his shot, adapting his stance and swing accordingly. A shooter should in essence follow the same routine in taking a shot, though he may have to reach a decision in a much shorter space of time. The important thing is that he must know how to 'play' the shot required, including such details as the need to look at the head because the target has length, so that he can devote his whole concentration to hitting the target. The best way to learn how to deal with various types of shot is to take lessons with a qualified instructor at a shooting school. You can learn from experience and your own mistakes, but it is a lengthy, and often rather heartbreaking process, which will not in my view compensate for the money you save. Until and unless you have acquired this foundation of shooting knowledge, you can never hope to be other than an erratic performer. However, when you have, you should with practice be able to develop your natural talents as a game shot to their fullest extent with every prospect of becoming a competent and consistent shot, who is welcome at any shoot.

Practice

I have already mentioned the importance of practice to the game shot, and do not propose to dwell further on it except to say that you cannot hope to do justice to yourself unless you make time for it, and this applies particularly to the young shot who is still striving to reach his full potential. In the next Chapter certain specific ways are discussed in which clay pigeon shooting can help to promote both knowledge and performance.

Fitness

Very few shooting men are alive to the advantages of being shooting fit at the start of a season. Rough shooters certainly appreciate that it is an asset to be generally physically fit, but more in relation to the walking they have to do than their actual shooting. Yet every time a 12-bore of $6\frac{1}{2}$lb, firing a standard load cartridge, recoils, the firer is subjected to a blow of approximately 100 ft/lb. per sec. As this is delivered at a low velocity of only about 15 ft per sec, it is barely noticed by the shooter. But if it is repeated a large number of times, when, for example, 100 or more cartridges are fired during a day, the cumulative effect combined with the effort required to lift the gun repeatedly to the shoulder exacts a significant physical toll. The less fit a shooter is, the more likely this is to prejudice his shooting.

I believe therefore it will well repay any shooter to take his gun out with a pair of snap caps into the garden, and practice his gun mounting drill for ten minutes or so daily, for two or three weeks before the season begins. If he can also take it with him on country walks when he exercises his dog, so much the better, because the more he can tone up his muscles, and familiarise them with the job they will have to do, the better they will serve him.

Although the visible cause of a miss may be head movement, or some such manifestation, I feel the underlying cause can often be, for example, indecision brought about by lack of knowledge of how to take a shot, or tiredness, or lack of practice, and that the part these three factors may play should be understood, so that the shooter can take steps to discount them.

Common Causes of Missing

In my experience the main causes of missing can be grouped under four headings:-

1. Head movement
2. Incorrect gun mounting
3. Premature gun mounting
4. Dithering on the aim.

I have mentioned some instances of these already, but as there is nothing more aggravating than a series of seemingly inexplicable misses, it may be helpful to summarise them here for easy reference.

The two most frequent manifestations of head movement are bobbing the head down to meet the stock as the gun is brought to the shoulder, and lifting the cheek off the stock just before the trigger is pulled. The former fault most often occurs when the shooter is looking down at his target, e.g. when you are shooting ground game or low flying birds, such as partridges or grouse. I have found myself doing it when shooting woodpigeon coming low to decoys. It induces the same effect as lowering the backsight of a rifle, that is, it causes the shot to go low. When shooting birds that are well up, it is unlikely to occur as the tendency then is for the shooter to raise his head, and bring the stock right up to it. The best way to check whether you have developed this fault is to load with snap caps, and 'shoot' at the reflection of your eye in a full length mirror, which will immediately reveal any head movement of this kind. It is sometimes a difficult habit of which to cure oneself if it has gone unchecked for any period; a possible cure might be to go and spend two or three evenings shooting high pigeon flighting into a wood.

Involuntarily lifting the head off the stock either just before, or just as the trigger is pulled is a rather different matter. It may be due to overeagerness to see your quarry killed, or a form of flinching induced by a bruised cheek, probably caused by firing too heavy a load in too light a gun. In the latter case the remedy is simply to use a lighter load. In that of the former the only cure is self-discipline.

Incorrect gun mounting can take many forms. Probably the two most common are mounting the butt insufficiently high on the shoulder, or on to the point of the shoulder and bicep; in the latter instance this may cause the shooter to cock his head over to meet the stock, further aggravating the error in aim. If your gun fits you correctly, faulty gun mounting should only be an isolated occurence due to hastiness, in which case it is nothing to worry about, or possibly lack of practice, when the remedy is obvious. If however it starts to become a frequent occurrence, you should have the fit checked, as it is likely to be due to too long a stock.

Premature gun mounting and its disastrous consequences have already been dealt with. From what I have seen, I would unhesitatingly say that it is the commonest cause of first barrel misses at high birds in general, and pheasants in particular. The only cure is to discipline yourself to wait until the bird has come sufficiently well in to allow you to mount the gun and shoot all in one smartly executed, spontaneous movement, similar to that used in hitting a ball.

Dithering on the aim before pulling the trigger is a fault to which inexperienced shots are prone. There are a number of causes, such as not trusting your eye at the last moment, the appearance of an unfamiliar target and uncertainty of how to deal with it, or lack of self-confidence. If you train yourself to trust your eye, and adopt the philosophy that it is better to take your shot well and miss, than to fluff around and fluke, you will soon master this fault, and have nothing to worry about.

There are of course various other reasons why people miss, such as curling the thumb or fingers of the left hand over the barrels so that the eyes do not register a true centreline as the muzzles come to bear on the target; mistiming your shot, or not looking at the head of your quarry. But generally if you think carefully over the four principal causes mentioned above, you will find one of them is the reason why you miss.

Miscellaneous Factors Affecting Missing

The first reaction of almost everyone when they miss is that they have done so behind. But surprising though it may seem, this is far from always the case. I have watched a man at a shooting school dealing with low incoming clays, whose complaint was that he was very off form that season. He had convinced himself that he had been missing consistently behind. As a result each time he mounted his gun he gave the barrels a hefty jerk, and missed every one of his first six clays well in front. When told this by the instructor he looked at him with bewilderment and disbelief. However he did what he was told, missed the next clay just in front, and then broke the following twelve in a row. In my view low flying quarry are missed at least as often in front as behind. So if you do have a bad patch of missing such birds, try, as I explained earlier, to shoot the pants off the next one, and you may well surprise yourself when it crumples, dead in the air.

High birds are more frequently missed behind, generally due to failure to look at the head and premature gun mounting, the cure for both of which needs no further explanation.

Occasionally a person's master eye may become tired and the other assume temporary dominance. This means in effect that his gun no longer fits, so that muzzles do not point where he is looking. I fancy I have once experienced this myself at the end of a long day's grouse shooting, when for no apparent reason I went right off form. The people most likely to be afflicted with this are those whose eyes are fairly equally matched. Fortunately it is a rare occurance, and if you can diagnose it in time, the cure is simply to blink the left, or other eye, as you take your shot. This phenomenon is known in America as 'cross shooting', and expert shots there try to take all sorts of precautions to obviate it, such as having a mid-way bead on the top rib as well as one at the muzzles; in my view this is making a mountain out of a molehill, and quite unnecessary.

There is no doubt that with age people's sight can change, and their ability to reach out with their arms diminish. When either or both these things happen, it will of course mean that the fit of your gun needs altering. In one case I know of, a person who had a 15 in. stock as a young man, had had it shortened progressively to $13\frac{1}{2}$ in. in his latter days, and remained a very useful shot. When people go off form in old age, they often attribute it to 'slowing up', and resign themselves to it, as something about which nothing can be done. Although age undoubtedly slows up a person's reactions, experience also brings its compensations, and it is certainly well worth having the fit of your gun checked periodically and adjusted as necessary. If you do this, you may surprise yourself and your friends with how little handicap your years have imposed. Even afflictions, such as partial loss of the use of an arm due to illness or injury, may be to a great extent discounted by changing to a lighter gun with shorter barrels and firing a lighter load. So if you start to miss for no apparently explicable reason, irrespective of whether you are young or old, never resign yourself to the situation; there is probably nothing wrong that a competent shooting instructor cannot cure, though in some cases it may be impracticable to make it a one hundred per cent cure.

9 how clays can help

General

There is a great deal of rubbish talked by some game shots about clay shooting, and by some clay shots about game shooting. Basically there is no reason why, if you are a good marksman at game, you cannot become an equally good one at clays, or vice versa. However you must appreciate that, for example, a down-the-line clay presents an entirely different target to a driven pheasant, and that in order to deal as successfully with the former as the latter you need time to play your eye in and master the different 'stroke' you have to make with your gun, because you are in effect facing a 'change of bowling'. It is because some people are not aware of this fundamental fact of shooting life that you may hear it alleged that clay shooting is bad for your game shooting, or clay shots do not make good game shots. Do not believe any such nonsense; there are many shooting men who are equally proficient marksmen at game and clays, and there is absolutely no reason why you cannot be so too, if you wish.

I hope this disposes of the myths and illusions on this score, that are bandied about in the shooting world, and may sow doubts in the mind of an aspiring game shot as to the wisdom of attending a shooting school. Practice at clays under the guidance of a qualified instructor is the best, and most humane way of learning how to become a competent game shot.

Shooting Schools and Practice Layouts

The number of shooting schools dispersed around the country is growing, but the coverage provided is still far from comprehensive. The instruction at some is based on the 'swing and intercept' method of shooting, by which in my view you will never be able to realise your full potential as a marksman, so I cannot recommend them. But if you can find one with a good instructor who teaches the instinctive method, which I have outlined in this book, then in my opinion it is certainly worth the time, trouble, and money you will have to spend on going there for a course of lessons. I fully appreciate that everyone will have to tailor what he can do in this respect according to the length of his purse. You should regard the outlay required as an investment in the future enjoyment of your sport. If you are prepared to spend, say, £500 on a gun, and an estimated £200 a year on your shooting for the next twenty years, this amounts to an expenditure of £4,500. It is surely worth investing £100 at the beginning of this period in learning how to shoot as well as you can, so that you obtain the best value for your money. In fact the larger the amount you feel able to devote to your sport, the greater the force of this argument. So unless it is genuinely impracticable, I do most strongly urge the aspiring game shot to start out by taking a course of lessons at a shooting-school. Even if it is only a short course of two or three, it will be invaluable in giving him a sound basis on which to build. Books of instruction, such as this, can help you to teach yourself to an extent dependent on the author's ability to give clear explanations, and yours to translate these into the correct actions. But in the final analysis there is no substitute for good practical instruction, even if it is only needed to put the polish on your performance, and only rarely is that the case. Success in home doctoring is limited by the patient's ability to diagnose correctly what has gone wrong. The same applies in principle to teaching yourself to shoot, so if you try to do so, and at any stage success appears to elude you, the sooner you consult a qualified practitioner the better, to ascertain what has gone wrong, and have it put right. If you don't, the fault may become habitual, and consequently extremely difficult to eradicate at a later stage.

Some people have a touching faith in the ability of gamekeepers to teach the young entry to shoot. Without intending any disrespect to that generally excellent body of men, in my experience such faith is more often than not misplaced, and the same holds good in the main of shooting men, who are themselves proficient marksmen. It is considered an essential qualification of an instructor that he should be able to see the shot column in the air. Very few, other than qualified shooting coaches, possess the knack, though it is not difficult to acquire. I have done so. But the more I have studied the question of teaching people how to shoot, the less importance I have come to attach to it, because if the trainee hits the target, it does not matter, and if he misses, the instructor has to look at him in order to find out why. So many amateur instructors, whom I have watched, simply glue their eyes to the clay, and then tell their pupil that he has missed one foot behind, or as the case may be, instead of checking that he has mounted the gun correctly, etc. so that they can put right the fault that has caused the miss. Another common failing of amateur instructors is to embark on a long dissertation about 'following up the smoke trail, and trying to shoot his brother in front'. This merely encourages the unfortunate pupil to take his eyes off the target, and shoot at points in space, so such hits as he achieves are a matter of chance instead of mastery of a sound technique. So a novice who is unable to attend a shooting school should be very wary in selecting a mentor from among his shooting friends. Really competent amateur instructors are rare birds indeed!

A great deal of useful practice as well as good fun can be had with a clay pigeon trap if it is well sited, so that a variety of different types of 'bird' can be shown. This is particularly the case if a few friends combine together to shoot in their spare time, so that they

144

can take it in turns to operate the trap, and also to act as critic of each other's shooting. If this latter is done intelligently and constructively it can be a real help to both parties in improving performance. We can all develop faults in technique of which we are unaware, such as 'rainbowing', or allowing the fingers of the left hand to encroach over the top of the right barrel, and these can be the source of a series of seemingly inexplicable misses, which is most frustrating. Yet a critical observer should be able to spot the error in a trice, and put us right. It is also a help to him because he learns the pitfalls into which he can just as easily slip when he is alone, and has to find his own salvation.

We all have certain shots which we find particularly difficult to master. A quite common one, for example, is a going away bird which is 'well up' or higher. From my own experience, I believe this is the exception that proves the rule, in that it is necessary consciously to aim in front. But again, if you trust your eye to tell you when you are 'on', and pull as soon as it does, such birds will come tumbling out of the sky just as readily as others. Practice at clays is the best way of learning how to deal with problem shots of this kind, because in essence the reason why you miss them is lack of self-confidence, stemming from lack of knowledge of how to deal with them. You often hear someone say 'I can never hit such-and-such a bird'. What he means is 'I don't know how to deal with such-and-such a target, so I just raise my gun, shoot, and hope for the best.'! Some shots are certainly more difficult than others, but all can be mastered equally well, if you have the will to do so. Unfortunately because of the aura of mystery with which game shooting has become surrounded, some people all too readily accept defeat. Don't; anyone, almost irrespective of age, who wants to be a competent shot, can become one.

Practice Layouts — Siting and Safety

The key to good sport and practice with clays is a first class trap. Electrically operated ones are too expensive, and too dependent on a handy source of power for general use in this context. The best of the hand operated ones are just as effective; also they are robust, simple to work, and if the maker's instructions are followed should give long and trouble-free service. They are easy to adjust to allow high or low, fast or slow 'birds' to be shown in singles or doubles, as desired. Unfortunately such traps have increased sharply in price in recent years. But their big advantage over cheaper models is their versatility, which is a very important consideration when you have a 'one-trap' layout, where a trap which only throws singles, and/or has no adjustment on the mainspring to control the speed of the clay can be a decided handicap. So if the cost of a new trap of the better kind is prohibitive for one person, it is well worth considering a joint purchase with a friend. Sometimes such traps can be obtained secondhand for a few pounds through advertisements in the local press, country house sales, and so on. If you acquire one by such means, especially if it is of a make with which you are not familiar, it is advisable to take two precautions. Firstly, have it overhauled by a qualified person, e.g. your local gunsmith, who if he cannot do it himself should be able to advise you who can. Secondly, obtain a copy of the maker's operating instructions. All clay pigeon traps have a powerful mainspring, and if mechanically defective, or incorrectly operated may cause serious injury, e.g. a broken arm.

Always make sure that the trapper, especially where this is a young person, is conversant with how to operate the trap, because the very simplicity of this may lead to a novice overlooking some elementary precaution, and giving himself, and probably you also, a nasty fright, if nothing worse!

To use a trap successfully and safely it must be affixed to a firm platform. This can be a balk of timber, such as an old railway sleeper, fastened to the ground with iron spikes, or a substantial concrete block. In these cases the bolts by which the base plate of the trap is secured should be countersunk in the platform. Where it is expedient to have a movable platform a heavy workbench or table may serve satisfactorily, or a welded iron frame of suitable design. Considerable stress is set up every time the trap is released, and to withstand the cumulative effect of this, whatever type of platform you decide upon must be both stable and robust. A permanent fixed platform has therefore obvious advantages, where practicable.

Selecting a suitable site is the next problem. A clay can go up to about 90 yds, dependent on the trap, the height from which it is launched, and the strength of the wind etc. Small shot can travel up to 250 yds or more before it is spent, so if you are shooting across open ground a danger area over an appropriate arc of 300 yds from the firing point should be allowed. Clays, or bits of them are not harmful to farm stock, but a whole one, or large piece can give a person quite a nasty thump, even when spent, if it hits him. These factors must therefore be taken into account when setting up a layout, as must provision of adequate protection for the trapper and trap. The needs of this last in each case are a matter for individual judgement and commonsense; if timber is used it should be faced with metal sheeting to prevent shot penetrating gaps in the planking; an earth bank can be satisfactory, but should be turfed over; if firing over the top of the trap is to take place, overhead cover will have to be provided. Where the trap house is dug into the ground some form of drainage may be necessary, and also flooring.

Ideally you should try to find a site that allows high, as well as low birds to be shown, such as a sharply rising piece of ground, an old chalk or sandpit. A hypothetical one-trap layout based on one of the latter is shown in *Diagram 64*. The trap house is at **X**, 20 yds back from the pit face. This allows high birds to be shown to anyone at stand **A**. By suitably organising the trap house, an occupant of butt **B** can shoot simulated incoming grouse or partridges, and if a gun stands beside the trap house at **X** he can be shown going away birds. Similarly by moving to one or other flank he can practise

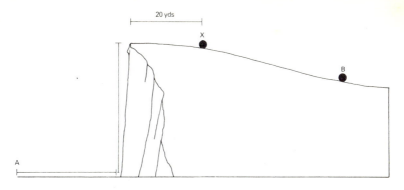

64. A versatile one-trap layout based on a disused quarry.

dealing with crossing birds. Achieving a multi-purpose layout like this does of course depend on having a clear all-round field of fire. But despite complications arising from farming operations, rights of way, and such like, it is surprising how easy it is to establish a layout on these lines, even if one owns no land one's self and is dependent on gaining the goodwill of a farmer. Shooting tenants can pose a problem. However again by the exercise of a little initiative and goodwill a satisfactory arrangement can often be made. There is one further factor which may have to be considered. Cottages in the country are being increasingly bought up by business men as 'second homes', to which they can come at week-ends, for holidays, or to live in retirement. They are apt to take exception to the noise of clay pigeon shooting, especially if this disturbs their afternoon siesta or Sunday morning slumber-in. Their objections, in my experience, usually stem from their failure to appreciate that the countryside is as much the countryman's place of work and play as the town is, or was theirs, and is not just an idyll of peace and solitude, where nothing ever happens. So although I firmly believe that countrymen have every right to enjoy themselves shooting clay pigeons whenever they wish, it may be tactful in certain circumstances to take prior steps to try to discount any objections of this kind likely to arise.

Finally, if you create an established layout over which you and your friends shoot regularly, it will be prudent to have insurance cover against injury to a third party, and damage to property.

Conclusion

Although you may be able to learn quite a lot of the elements of gun handling and shooting at home, there will come a time, when, if you wish to become a really useful marksman, you will need more expert tuition and better facilities. These are best obtained at a shooting school by having a course of lessons under a qualified instructor. To gain full value from this, you must practise what you have been taught in order to perfect the coordination of the actions of hands and eyes so that you can perform these instinctively and fluently in the field. As I have tried to show, it should not be too difficult by the exercise of a little initiative to organise your own practice clay layout for this purpose, especially if you can find a few friends willing to help. Try to include a 'plate' in your layout, so that you can see the patterns shot by your gun(s). Some people may laugh this idea to scorn, but it can enable you to obtain a lot of useful information about patterns, and also learn for yourself the truth about some of the hoary old myths you will undoubtedly hear about cartridges.

Any top golfer will tell you that it is not the spectacularly long drive off the tee that wins holes, but the good short game near, and on the green. Similarly in game shooting it is not the gallery shot at the high bird that fills the bag, but the ability consistently to kill the so-called easy birds. Remember, one of the main objects of practice at shooting, as in other sports and games, is to build up self-confidence, and nothing stimulates this more than success. So a good practice layout should have provision for showing relatively easy targets as well as difficult ones.

Practice at clays can genuinely help to improve your game shooting, and at the same time provide a lot of fun for yourself and your friends.

10 how to shoot your best all the time

If you wish to develop your natural talents as a marksman with a shotgun to the full, a good start is invaluable. It will help you to achieve this if you accept the following six points as your guide lines to the path you should follow:-

(a) A shotgun is a lethal weapon and must at all times be handled safely, and should be seen to be so.

(b) A sound elementary knowledge of how your gun and cartridge function, together with their capabilities is a positive aid to obtaining best value from them.

(c) It is necessary to shoot with a gun which fits you, because it points where you are looking when correctly mounted to the shoulder.

(d) Shooting moving targets with a shotgun is essentially a matter of coordination of hands and eyes, so you must therefore know:-

    (i)   How to position and use your eyes.

    (ii) How to hold the gun with your hands, and use them to take various shots.

    (iii) How to place and use your feet to assist your hands and eyes in performing their function.

(e) Sound basic instruction in how to shoot, and practice at putting this into effect are just as necessary to good marksmanship, as to good play at golf or cricket.

(f) The wider the knowledge you can acquire of all the quarry you pursue, and other related matters, the better the sport you will be able to enjoy.

The arguments on which these precepts are based have been discussed in detail in the preceding chapters, so the force of them should be fully appreciated. They should provide the aspiring game shot with a sound foundation on which to build a fuller understanding of his sport, and of the spirit that should motivate him as a sportsman.

If you take a lively and intelligent interest in all that happens in the field, you will find that the experience you gain is a great help in enabling you to make the most of your opportunities. This applies very obviously to rough shooting, where you have to rely on your own and your dog's wits to get on terms with your quarry, whatever that may be. But it can also prove no less valuable when you are standing in the line having birds driven to you, especially in being alert to chances that others miss because they are caught napping. As you grow older it may save you a lot of abortive walking by

149

assisting you to pick the right place and be there at the right time. It will teach you that it never pays to be in haste. If a line of guns and beaters goes too fast game is walked over, flushes behind, and escapes. If scenting conditions are difficult even a good dog takes time to puzzle out a line and find and flush the quarry, or make its retrieve. You will learn that many a bird, allegedly fallen dead, turns out to be a strong runner, and that in such cases it pays to trust your dog, whatever 'helpful' suggestions others may offer. If you keep alert and watchful, you will be able to gain a lot from experience to help you fill the bag.

As I said at the beginning of this book, game shooting is a recreation, and so our aim is to enjoy it. But we will only achieve this if we take an interest in all aspects of our sport, so that we can appreciate a day's shooting for its quality rather than the quantity of game in the bag at the end of it. An important part in this is unquestionably played by a person becoming a competent enough marksman to gain a sense of achievement from his own participation. The primary purpose of this book has been to help you in this respect. I believe that if you follow the instructions in these pages, you will become able to shoot your best, and when, through practice, the 'drill' has grown instinctive, you should be capable of continuing to do so to the end of your sporting career. But never forget that earning a reputation as a 'good shot' involves much more than just becoming a polished performer with the gun.

Finally, I will leave you with this thought; after completing a masterly approach to your objective there is nothing more infuriating and frustrating than to be denied the fruits of victory by one's own failure to bring matters to a successful conclusion. Yet this is the fate every shooter begs for himself who does not take the trouble to learn to become as effective a marksman as his natural abilities allow.

appendix: some metric equivalents for the shooter

1. **Barrel Lengths**
   25 in. = 63.50 cm.
   26 in. = 66.04 cm.
   27 in. = 68.58 cm.
   28 in. = 71.12 cm.
   29 in. = 73.66 cm.
   30 in. = 76.20 cm.

2. **Cast-off/Bend**
   $\frac{1}{16}$ in. = 1.6 mm.
   $\frac{1}{8}$ in. = 3.2 mm.
   $\frac{1}{4}$ in. = 6.4 mm.
   $\frac{3}{8}$ in. = 9.5 mm.
   $\frac{1}{2}$ in. = 12.7 mm.
   $\frac{3}{4}$ in. = 19.1 mm.
   1 in. = 25.4 mm

3. **Chamber Lengths**
   2 in. = 50 mm. *
   $2\frac{1}{2}$ in. = 65 mm. *
   $2\frac{3}{4}$ in. = 70 mm. *
   3 in. = 75 mm. *
   (* Figures used in the Gun Trade.)

4. **Bore Diameters**
   4-Bore : .938 in. = 2.37 cm.
   8-Bore : .835 in. = 2.02 cm.
   10-Bore : .775 in. = 1.97 cm.
   12-Bore : .729 in. = 1.82 cm.
   16-Bore : .662 in. = 1.68 cm.
   20-Bore : .615 in. = 1.56 cm.
   28-Bore : .550 in. = 1.40 cm.
   .410   : .410 in. = 1.04 cm.

5. The 40-yd equivalent for patterning is 35 m., i.e. 38.3 yds.

6. **Shot Loads**

Ounces	Grammes
$1\frac{5}{8}$	46
$1\frac{1}{2}$	42.5
$1\frac{1}{4}$	35.5
$1\frac{3}{16}$	34
$1\frac{1}{8}$	32
$1\frac{1}{16}$	30
1	28.5
$1\frac{5}{16}$	26.5
$\frac{7}{8}$	25
$1\frac{3}{16}$	23
$\frac{5}{8}$	17.5
$\frac{9}{16}$	16
$\frac{7}{16}$	12.5
$\frac{5}{16}$	9

Index

Figures in italics refer to illustrations